Emotional Abuse Workbook

A Life-Changing Guide to Overcome Anxiety, Heartache, Flashbacks, Confusion and Rebuild Your Self-Esteem

D1715046

Dr. Theresa J.Covert

Table of contents

Introduction
How to use this book

Y ou probably picked up this workbook because you have some experience with emotional abuse. Whether you are currently in an
emotionally abusive relationship, or have been in one and are trying to
recover from it, this workbook will be your guiding light to healing and
ensuring you do not get trapped in an abusive cycle ever again.

Emotional abuse is not talked about as often, so it can be difficult to
know how to recover from it. You might be feeling helpless, scared,
angry, depressed, anxious, ashamed and/or insecure. I am here to tell
you that your feelings are completely valid. You have been through a
lot. Being in a toxic relationship can drain the happiness out of you,
leaving you struggling to keep your head above the water.

If you are a victim of emotional abuse and are struggling to navigate
through your relationship, this workbook will give you the right guidance and strength to take back control of your life. Working through
this book will provide you with the best strategies to handle the relationship, and also help you learn to love yourself so that you do not
tolerate any more abuse.

This workbook will dive into the warning signs of an emotionally abusive relationship, provide you with tips on how to handle (or leave)
your partner, guide you on how to take back control of your life, and
finally provide you with the tools needed to heal and love yourself.
Each chapter has exercises that drive you to reflect in a manner that
helps you to express your emotions, evaluate your situation and eventually decide what you want in your life.

Take your time. You have been through a lot and there may be a great
deal of emotions you have bottled up within you. As you go through
this workbook, break down the emotional barriers you may have made
for yourself and let all your feelings spill out onto the pages. Transfer-
ring your thoughts and emotions out onto paper helps you relieve your

mind and body of the heavy burden you may carry. In addition to investigating your relationship, this workbook is also here to act as a therapeutic journal for you. Releasing your emotions through writing is a wonderful way to lighten your heartache.

Try to be as consistent as possible. As long as you regularly take some time in the day to focus on healing, you will feel stronger and more autonomous in no time. Read through the workbook keeping your life in mind, so that you can easily identify the pain-points specific to your relationship. The goal of the exercises is to allow you to pour out your thoughts and feelings without holding back. As you write down your responses, re-read your answers and sit with them. Take the time to reflect on what you have written, as this will provide clarity into how you want to navigate through your relationship from thereon.

Take a deep breath in. Exhale out all your worries and fears. This book is only here to help you and give you strength. You can do this.

Let's get started.

Part 1
Emotional Abuse

T he first section of this workbook unravels the truth about emotional abuse, starting with its warning signs. Are you sure you fully recognize what emotional abuse is? There may be some signals that you did not consider to be emotionally abusive, but in reality, very much are. There is also an emotional abuse test for you to complete, so that you can determine how many of the abusive signs your relationship encompasses.

You will also learn about the effects of emotional abuse. If you think you are in a toxic relationship, chances are you are familiar with some of these effects already. This section will dig deeper into the various ramifications of abuse and what further damage they can do if they continue to go unchecked.

It is imperative to know what healthy relationships look like, so that you can compare your relationship to a healthy relationship model and see where it is thriving, and where it is lacking. To explain this, there is a chapter outlining the differences between healthy and unhealthy relationships. Understanding the contrasts can truly open your eyes to determine whether or not your relationship is toxic.

Lastly, being able to identify toxic people is a skill that will prove useful to you in life, not just with your partner, but with other people you meet as you go about your journey. Not to say that you should completely avoid toxic people, but this particular chapter will educate you on how to know if someone is toxic and how to deal with them without putting yourself under emotional stress.

Part 1 of this workbook will enlighten you with an abundance of knowledge that will become part of your wellness toolbox moving forward. Knowing all the information and all the signs will be the first step to prioritizing yourself and healing.

Let's dive in.

Chapter 1
What is emotional abuse?

I f you have picked up this workbook, chances are you are probably unsure of whether you are currently in or have been in an emotionally abusive relationship, or you are seeking to learn more about what emotional abuse is. Either way, emotional abuse is a topic that is not talked about enough, and can seem like a grey area to most. Therefore, learning about it is extremely important, as it can save you or someone you know from a tremendous amount of pain.

When the world talks about abuse, most of the time, we hear about physical, verbal or sexual abuse rather than emotional abuse. Part of the reason may be because it is easier to identify the signs, and scars, of those types of abuse. When it comes to emotional abuse, this is where the waters get a bit murky. People are not as informed of the warning signs of emotional abuse, and are unable to identify whether they are a victim to this particular sort of abuse. Physical and emotional abuse are both unacceptable and traumatic, but unfortunately emotional abuse can be disguised easier than physical abuse through several tactics.

The commonality between physical and emotional abuse is the abuser wanting to control the other person. The most common reason for this need to gain control is due to the abuser most probably having been abused in their own childhood. They most likely grew up in a household observing their primary caregiver exhibit emotionally abusive behaviour and assumed this was "normal". Abuse is a learned behaviour from childhood and can be difficult to shake when one grows throughout their life. As the abusers grow up, they come across situations in their life that they are unable to deal with in a healthy manner, and so resort to controlling people or situations in order to deal with the discomfort they feel within themselves. Since people are not as aware of the signs of emotional abuse, the abuser's behaviour and reactions go unchecked and are reinforced over the years, causing them to believe that this behaviour is the norm.

An emotional abuser is the puppet master of their partner's mind. If you have any experience with an emotionally abusive partner, you are probably familiar with this. They dictate how you conduct your own life, down to the very last detail, whether it be how you talk, who you meet, what you say, and so on. The abuser gets into your head in various ways and somehow convinces you to live your life based on the abuser's terms. The terrifying part about being the victim of emotional abuse is sometimes not knowing just how much damage this can do biologically, socially, psychologically and sometimes even financially.

Emotional abusers do not respect other people. Period. They disregard your autonomy - your freedom to think, speak, behave in a certain way, feel, etc. There is no mutual understanding in this type of relationship - instead of driving down a two-way highway, the relationship drives down a one-way street, heading towards the direction of only the abuser's needs.

Below are some of the ways that abusers dominate their partners, and will be discussed in great detail throughout this workbook:

Push boundaries

When an emotional abuser wants something to go their way, they will stop at nothing to control the outcome. They will not take no for an answer, and will therefore test your boundaries to get what they seek. To an abuser, the word "no" signifies defiance, which ultimately makes them feel as though they are losing control. This does not sit well with them at all; therefore, they force you to lower your boundaries so that they can change that "no" to a "yes".

Passive-aggressive behaviour

This type of behaviour is more subtle, as it involves the abuser hurting you without showing outright aggression. Snarky remarks, insults and dismissive body language are all examples of passive-aggressiveness, and can sometimes be difficult to spot. The abuser's goal here is to gain their control by making you feel lesser than them, without making it too obvious.

Invalidate your feelings

Most of the time, if not all the time, abusers rarely validate your feelings. They disregard your emotions, needs, opinions and accomplishments because they are not as important as the abuser's own needs. The abuser is too self-absorbed with what they want and need, that nobody else's needs are ever usually addressed. They may listen to what you have to say, but will hardly hear it and process it. This is mainly because the abuser's feelings were not validated as a child and so they never felt heard. As a result, the abuser is not programmed to listen to someone else's feelings and in turn does not hear them either. This blocks good communication from entering the relationship and you may be left feeling invisible.

Silent treatment

This is a form of punishment the abuser uses when you do not give them what they want, or when they feel like they are unable to control you. By completely shutting you out, and if you are codependent on them or have a codependent personality, they know this form of punishment will push you into a negative emotional spiral and will probably make you disregard your own needs, to a point where you agree to do anything to get back their attention.

Ignore you

This may seem bizarre, but emotional abusers sometimes also blatantly ignore you when you speak or do anything. Due to their self-absorbed nature, they oftentimes subconsciously do not even realize what you might be saying or doing.

Aggression

If an abuser does not get what they want, or they feel as though they are not able to control you, they can get aggressive. This doesn't always mean physical abuse, per se, it also refers to verbal abuse, screaming and hurtful insults. They start acting like a bully and tear you down until you give in to their demands.

Manipulation

Since the emotional abuser's goal is to get what they want, they will use several manipulation tactics to get inside your head. What is dangerous about this is that they are usually able to make you believe that you made a decision on your own, without any influence from them. This can lead to the abuser absolving any responsibility for manipulating you, should anything go wrong. The abuser is satisfied, as they get what they want through control, while you are made to believe that you were and are in total control of your own decisions.

Gaslighting

Gaslighting entails making someone doubt their own reality. If you feel a certain way, or know something happened in a particular fashion, the abuser will use gaslighting as a way to convince you that your reality is inaccurate. If you happen to have low self-esteem or low sense of self-worth, you will fall for it and start to question your reality. As a result, you will believe your partner's truth and disregard your own. You may conclude that your feelings are invalid, or that you are remembering things wrong. Someone with low self-esteem/low self-worth usually succumbs to this out of fear of losing their partner (the abuser).

After exhibiting all of these abusive behaviours, the abuser rarely takes any responsibility for the damage they have caused. An apology is not in their vocabulary, as they genuinely do not think what they are doing is wrong.

Has your partner done any of these things to you? Write down examples of when each of these may have happened to you.

Pushed your boundaries

_____
_____
_____
_____
_____
_____
_____
_____
_____
_____
_____
_____

Been passive-aggressive

_____
_____
_____
_____
_____
_____
_____
_____
_____
_____
_____

Invalidated your feelings

_____

_____

_____

_____

_____

_____

_____

_____

_____

_____

_____

_____

_____

_____

Give you the silent treatment

_____

_____

_____

_____

_____

_____

_____

_____

_____

_____

_____

_____

_____

_____

Ignored you

_____
_____
_____
_____
_____
_____
_____
_____
_____
_____
_____
_____

Been aggressive

_____
_____
_____
_____
_____
_____
_____
_____
_____
_____
_____
_____
_____
_____

Manipulated you

_____
_____
_____
_____
_____
_____
_____
_____
_____
_____
_____
_____
_____

Gaslighted you

_____
_____
_____
_____
_____
_____
_____
_____
_____
_____
_____
_____
_____

Emotional Abuse Test

L et's take a second to absorb the information you just read and wrote. You may be familiar with a lot of these signs, or these signs may be a revelation for you. Either way, now that you have a brief idea of the warning signs of emotional abuse, it is time to take the emotional abuse test. If you know that you are in an emotionally abusive relationship, this test should be relatively straightforward for you to answer. The purpose of this test is to evaluate which areas of your relationship determine its abusive nature, and the intensity of each.

As you read through the statements, take your time to reflect on your own relationship. You are not on a time limit, unlike most other tests, so feel free to really introspect. You will be asked to evaluate the statements by rating how strongly and how often you experience these signs on a scale of 0-2; 0 being rarely, 1 being sometimes and 2 being all the time. Circle the rating that best describes your relationship. Quantifying your experiences will help you look at how abusive your relationship actually is from a more logical perspective too. The higher your total score is, the more likely it is that you are in an emotionally abusive relationship. A higher score will also show you how intense the abuse can get.

In addition to providing a rating, you will be asked to write down examples of times you have experienced these signs. The purpose of writing these episodes down is to vent about what you go through in your relationship without feeling afraid. Like the rest of this workbook, this test is designed to allow you to express yourself, as well as determine the intensity of the emotional abuse you endure.

Feel free to start whenever you are ready.

1. *I am afraid to talk about certain topics with my partner*

                    0   *1*   *2*

Examples:

_____

_____

_____

_____

_____

_____

_____

_____

2. *My partner humiliates me in front of other people*

                    0   *1*   *2*

Examples:

_____

_____

_____

_____

_____

_____

_____

3. *My partner tries to control my life*

              0   *1*   *2*

Examples:

_____

_____

_____

_____

_____

_____

_____

_____

4. *My partner makes me believe that my stories or my perspective are not accurate or important*

              0   *1*   *2*

Examples:

_____

_____

_____

_____

_____

_____

_____

_____

5. **My partner blames me and other people for their mistakes or problems**

0   1   2

Examples:

_____

_____

_____

_____

_____

_____

_____

6. **My partner gets aggressive with me if I disagree with them or reject them**

0   1   2

Examples:

_____

_____

_____

_____

_____

_____

_____

_____

_____

7. *My partner manipulates me to give them what they want, even when I do not feel comfortable doing so*

0   1   2

Examples:

_____
_____
_____
_____
_____
_____
_____
_____
_____
_____

8. *My partner makes me feel like I am not good enough*

0   1   2

Examples:

_____
_____
_____
_____
_____
_____
_____
_____
_____
_____

9. *My partner uses the silent treatment as a form of punishment*

                        0   *1*   *2*

Examples:

_____

_____

_____

_____

_____

_____

_____

_____

_____

10. *I feel like our whole relationship revolves around my partner and my needs are hardly ever met*

                        0   *1*   *2*

Examples:

_____

_____

_____

_____

_____

_____

_____

_____

_____

11. I fear my partner's reactions to certain things

0   1   2

Examples:

_____

_____

_____

_____

_____

_____

_____

_____

_____

_____

12. My partner gets jealous when I interact with or talk about someone other than them

0   1   2

Examples:

_____

_____

_____

_____

_____

_____

_____

_____

_____

_____

_____

Total score = ___ */24*

Good job on completing the test! It is commendable that you were able to reflect so deeply on these aspects of your relationship. It might have even been painful for you, but your strength in doing so is allowing you to take an important first step to helping yourself heal. If you have a score of 10 or more, you are probably in an emotionally abusive relationship. The higher your score is above 10, the more abusive your relationship is.

Based on your score and the examples you have recited, how emotionally abusive do you think your relationship is? Take some time to think about this.

If you believe that your relationship is emotionally abusive, do not worry. This workbook is specifically written to provide you with strength, motivation and guidance on how to maneuver through (or out of) this relationship.

Effects of emotional abuse

Unfortunately, the world sometimes forgets that the invisible scars born from emotional abuse are just as traumatic as those from physical abuse. We may not be able to see those wounds, but they can do serious damage to its victims. Emotional abuse can change the way someone sees the world, their brain chemistry and formation, and their susceptibility to mental illness.

Being constantly dominated by an emotional abuser is exhausting - it can leave you feeling vulnerable, powerless, scared and sometimes even worthless. Abusers have a way of ripping away your sense of control, almost as if someone were snatching away the remote control of your life.

Emotional abuse doesn't always pertain to couples, children raised by emotionally abusive parents are as susceptible, if not more, to these negative effects. There can be severe biological impact on a child suffering from emotional abuse from a young age, well into their adulthood. When someone is being abused, the stress hormone, cortisol, is released in the body due to chronic stress. Small amounts of cortisol are necessary for our survival, as it aids the "flight or fight" response, and equips us with the ability to stay alive in the face of danger. However, chronic stress leads to an over-release of cortisol over a long period of time, and this can negatively affect the brain and the body.

Exposure to emotional abuse at a young age can damage and prevent the development of the hippocampus - the center of the brain responsible for learning and memory. As a result of the smaller hippocampus size, the victim may have some trouble processing new information. Abuse and neglect can also result in underdevelopment of the corpus callosum, which is in charge of emotions, impulses and arousal. The growth of the cerebellum also gets stunted, which affects coordination and motor skills. Since abuse triggers highly emotional responses from the victim, there is increased activity in the amygdala - the part of the brain which is responsible for emotion regulation and behaviour - which impairs the victim's ability to control emotional outbursts. Because of this, a victim could have an overreaction to a non-harmful/non-threatening situation in their life, as their mind is constantly looking out for threats.

Childhood emotional abuse also tends to affect the growth of the medial lobe, temporal lobe and prefrontal cortex, depreciating the victim's ability to accurately assess their emotions and behaviours, and be self-aware. As a result, adult women in particular, may have strong reactions to certain triggers and will not be able to recognize the reason for their reaction due to the lack of self-awareness.

Victims experiencing emotional abuse often isolate themselves in order to "feel safe", and this can stagnate the growth of neural connections between different sections of the brain. Studies have shown that young adults who were bullied had less neural connections between the left and right hemispheres of the brain. The lack of fully-formed connections can lead to hostility, anger, depression, anxiety, PTSD, disassociation and sometimes drug abuse in the victim, showing that emotional abuse can severely affect the victim's ability to process and express emotions effectively.

Although these effects are not seen on the body through physical injuries, they are just as dire. It is essential to recognize the warning signs of emotional abuse and be aware of the negative impact it has on the body and brain, so that you can save yourself from these ramifications. It is a form of trauma that people are still struggling to identify and process, and can leave them feeling helpless. This is not to say that one cannot be healed from the trauma of abuse - there are several ways to restore the mind once the wounds are recognized. Determination to heal is usually the first step.

Chapter 2
Healthy vs. unhealthy relationships

E very relationship is different - each one has its own beauty, as well as its own imperfections. Since the dawn of mankind, human beings have survived and thrived due to social companionship - whether those are through tribes, communities, families or partners.

It is in our nature to seek companionship in order to feel safe and fulfilled, and romantic relationships are often the most sought out form of companionship. People usually crave having someone to share things with and to grow old with; knowing they have someone in their corner.

The basis of being in a relationship is usually to find true love, a great friend, and happiness. However, like most things in life, relationships also come with their own challenges. At the end of the day, even though a relationship entails two souls coming together to care for each other and love each other, these souls are still individual people with their own personalities, core values and beliefs.

No matter how similar or different these two people are, the way they conduct and maintain their relationship will determine whether or not it is a healthy one.

It is sometimes confusing to know whether the relationship you are in is in fact healthy or unhealthy. Each person has their own preferences, tolerances, vices, etc.

Who is to say what the universal definition of a happy relationship is? While the meaning of a happy relationship may differ person to person, there are a number of universal truths that determine whether your relationship is healthy or unhealthy:

1. *Being content within yourself*

In order to have a healthy relationship with someone else, you need to have a healthy relationship with yourself first. This means loving yourself unconditionally and feeling whole. It all starts with you.

We are constantly growing and changing, but before we get into a relationship with somebody, we should know who we are, what we want from life and what we want in a relationship.

We should feel confident about ourselves and be willing to be our authentic selves with another person. Being content with yourself means being able to validate yourself, instead of seeking validation from someone else.

Two people whose glasses are completely full can only add value to the relationship, since they are happy with themselves and do not need someone else to fill up their glass.

If you aren't whole and happy with yourself, your glass is only half full. If two people come together expecting the other person to fill up their glass, they may be disappointed, as the other person may not have that much to give from their glass either.

This can turn into an unhealthy codependent relationship that exhausts both parties.

How would you describe yourself as a person? What are your goals, core values, beliefs, your personality type?

_____

_____

_____

_____

_____

_____

_____

_____

_____

_____

_____

_____

What makes you happy? What do you want from life?

_____

_____

_____

_____

_____

_____

_____

_____

_____

_____

_____

What do you expect from your partner?

_____

_____

_____

_____

_____

_____

_____

_____

_____

_____

_____

_____

What are you looking for in a relationship?

_____

_____

_____

_____

_____

_____

_____

_____

_____

_____

Does your partner embody what you are looking for?

_____

_____

_____

_____

_____

_____

_____

_____

_____

_____

_____

2. *Understanding what true love actually looks like*

Love is a concept that many of us wish to bring to life, but may not fully understand. We might think we know what true love is based on past relationships, romance movies and novels, or simply from what people tell us. What true love actually is, is a choice. It is the choice we make to love someone whole-heartedly every day. While love is based on emotion, a choice is based on logic and reason. It is easy to fall in love with someone quickly because your emotions take over and you are addicted to that temporary feeling of happiness. However, once the romance and honeymoon period fades, which it will, true love will be determined by your CHOICE to keep loving this person through thick and thin. A choice based on reason and logic.

The foundation of a healthy relationship is friendship. If we can choose to remain close to our best friends, we can apply the same principle to our relationships - we can choose to love them every day, come what may. No relationship will constantly be magical and perfect, there will be times when you really question whether you want to keep going. At those times, the relationships that survive are the ones that are built from two people choosing to truly love each other every day regardless. True love is when two people consciously know everything about each other (the good and the flaws) and still choose to love each other and be with each other. Of course, this does not mean that you forgive your partner for abusive behaviour and choose to stay with them regardless of how they treat you. True love also means respecting each other, and if you are not being respected then your relationship is probably not very healthy.

If you ever asked an elderly couple what kept them together all these years, they would probably say it is acceptance and understanding. They have made the decision to be with each other, taking into consideration every single aspect of the other person. They have accepted who their partner is and they understand the way they operate. Only when you are able to accept and understand the other person, are you able to use your logical reasoning to decide whether you want to be with this person. Paradoxically, logic is what makes your love true and pure.

Describe your current or most recent relationship. Do you think it is/was based on true love?

_____

_____

_____

_____

_____

_____

_____

_____

_____

_____

What does true love mean to you?

3. *Accepting your partner for who they truly are*

Healthy relationships involve two people loving each other whole-heartedly, which means that they also accept each other for the way they are.

The first step is to accept yourself, flaws and all. Self-love is the key to having a healthy relationship with someone else. If you are able to accept yourself, you can be content within yourself.

When you are content from within, you are capable of accepting your partner for the way they are and will not expect them to change either.

Of course, if there are tiny aspects about your partner (or about you) that can be talked about and changed for the betterment of the relationship, that is totally understandable and healthy.

However, if you are unhappy with who your partner is at their very core, in terms of their values, beliefs and personality, you are going to have an unhappy relationship because you will constantly try to change them.

This can lead to consistent disappointment and feeling short-changed, while your partner could feel resentment towards you and insecure with themselves.

If you truly love someone for who they are, you would not want to change them. It is as simple as that.

What qualities about yourself do you accept? What qualities do you not wish to accept?

_____

_____

_____

_____

_____

_____

_____

_____

_____

_____

_____

_____

Do you accept your partner for who they are? Describe some of their traits (admirable and flaws).

_____

_____

_____

_____

_____

_____

_____

_____

_____

_____

_____

_____

Which of your partner's traits have you tried to change? How have you tried to change them?

_____

_____

_____

_____

_____

_____

_____

_____

_____

_____

_____

_____

_____

_____

_____

_____

_____

_____

_____

_____

_____

_____

_____

_____

_____

_____

4. *Being honest and respectful*

This goes without saying - honesty and respect are extremely vital in a healthy relationship. When you and your partner are able to be completely honest with each other and respect each other in every way, only then will your relationship make you feel secure and happy. When you both are honest with each other, you are coming from a place of emotional maturity. There will be times when the truth may not be something either of you want to hear, but the fact that it is being laid out shows that you respect each other and you want what is best for the other person.

Open communication is essential to making your relationship work, and if honesty is met with an emotional reaction, that may harm your relationship more than help. When someone is being honest with you, they are taking a big step and letting you in on the truth, even when it may hurt. By doing this, they are respecting you enough to make sure you are not sitting in the dark, oblivious to the truth. They believe that you are able to handle the truth and that they are able to tell you anything. At this point, it is best to show that person respect, rather than react with emotion, because they are taking a big step by being honest.

In emotionally abusive relationships, when the abuser is feeling insecure or reacts with emotion, they exhibit defensiveness to the person being honest and this usually results in a conflict, as they perceive this honesty to be an attack on their character. These kinds of arguments are based solely on insecurity and emotional reaction, when the conversation should be a healthy discussion about what was said. The more someone reacts to honesty rather than listens, the less their partner will be inclined to be honest in the future, as they will gravitate towards avoiding conflict. This is where relationships become toxic and unhealthy, as couples start to hide things from each other. Thus, it is important that partners respect each other and take a few breaths before responding to whatever is being said, so that a productive and positive conversation can take place.

Write down two examples of when your partner may have felt attacked and did not respect your honesty.

_____

_____

_____

_____

_____

_____

_____

_____

_____

_____

_____

_____

What is the level of honesty you and your partner have with each other? Why do you have this level of honesty?

_____

_____

_____

_____

_____

_____

_____

_____

_____

_____

_____

How does your partner show you respect (or disrespect)?

_____

_____

_____

_____

_____

_____

_____

_____

_____

_____

_____

Write down some episodes of when you were afraid to be honest with your partner because of how they might react.

_____

_____

_____

_____

_____

_____

_____

_____

_____

_____

_____

5. *There should be mutual trust*

Trust is the glue that holds the relationship together. If you do not trust each other, then you do not have a healthy relationship. Being committed to someone, means sharing a big part of your life with this person. Aspects of your life become intertwined and this person becomes extremely important to you.

If you do not trust them, either because of their character or because of emotional wounds you may have yet to heal, that could lead to a lot of pain. If you get anxious when your partner goes out with their friends without you, or you check their phone regularly, then you have low levels of trust in your partner.

The next step would be to figure out why you have such little trust in them. Have they done something in the past to break your trust? Do you have emotional wounds that you have not healed yet? Have you grown up watching your parents lack trust for each other?

Identifying why you may not trust them can help you resolve those issues and move past them. If your partner has given you legitimate reasons to not trust them and is not willing to work on earning your trust back, then you may need to do some thinking.

Mutual trust brings partners closer together, as both of you feel secure and safe with the other person. If this is not the case, you both can try to build your trust for the other. However, this only works if both partners are willing to work at it and be understanding of the other person's vulnerabilities.

Why do you or why don't you trust your partner?

_____

_____

_____

_____

_____

_____

_____

_____

_____

_____

_____

_____

Why does or why doesn't your partner trust you?

_____

_____

_____

_____

_____

_____

_____

_____

_____

_____

_____

Recount two incidents when you did not trust your partner and that led to an argument.

_____

_____

_____

_____

_____

_____

_____

_____

_____

_____

Recount two incidents when your partner did not trust you and that led to an argument.

_____

_____

_____

_____

_____

_____

_____

_____

_____

_____

_____

6. *Taking responsibility for your own feelings*

Your partner will most likely push your buttons and it is important to recognize when this happens. In a healthy relationship, you should be able to take responsibility for what you are thinking and how you are feeling, because you and only you are in charge of how you react to situations. For example, if your partner hurls a hurtful comment at you and you get upset, the first step is to recognize that getting upset is the reaction you chose to have. It is okay to feel what you feel, but from there, it is vital to think about what you can do to relieve that emotion or thought - whether it is taking some space to cool off or talking to your partner about it in a constructive manner.

Unhealthy relationships involve the person who has been hurt to blame their partner for their feelings. Their partner may be the trigger or the situation that caused them to have a reaction, but they did not dictate how the person should have felt, and vice versa. The person is choosing to feel this way, and also choosing whether they want to sit in that feeling, or to find a way to resolve it and let it go. It's not the easiest thing to do, but with practice, it becomes an automatic behaviour.

While taking responsibility for your own feelings, you both also need to be empathetic and understanding of the other person's feelings. If one person invalidates or disregards the other person's feelings, this can lead to the other person feeling unheard and unhappy, which is not the basis of a healthy relationship. Emotional abusers will also likely not take ownership for how they feel, because they do not know how to process their emotions. If you are able to process yours and take ownership for them, you have won half the battle. However, if your partner is unable to validate your feelings, then that is an issue you need to bring up with them.

When was the last time your partner did not take responsibility for their feelings and instead blamed you?

_____

_____

_____

_____

_____

_____

_____

_____

_____

_____

_____

How do you and your partner resolve emotional conflicts together?

_____

_____

_____

_____

_____

_____

_____

_____

_____

_____

_____

Do you think your partner respects and understands how you feel? Why/why not?

_____

_____

_____

_____

_____

_____

_____

_____

_____

_____

_____

_____

_____

_____

_____

_____

_____

_____

_____

_____

_____

_____

_____

7. *Making the relationship a priority*

The beginnings of a relationship, or the "honeymoon phase", is a sweet period where a couple gets lost in each other and puts in the most amount of effort to get to know each other. The relationship feels super exciting and they both cannot get enough of each other.

You are probably familiar with this honeymoon phase, as you probably felt that rush of infatuation at the beginning of your relationship. Once the excitement dies down though, some couples tend to reduce the effort they make to maintain their relationship. A healthy relationship means constantly making it a priority - that means consistently making your partner feel loved, wanted and important, however that looks like for you.

This is when you both are a team. Both partners make equal effort to remind their partner of how much they mean to them. It is important to be selfless here and perform acts of giving, so that your partner knows you truly care.

When someone does not make their relationship a priority, it can make the other partner feel invisible, especially when they are giving more than they are receiving. Feelings of resentment, despair, frustration and sadness are regular visitors for this person and this leads to an unhealthy equation with their partner.

If you think you are giving too much and not receiving as much, that probably means your partner is more absorbed with what they need and are not considering what you need. In healthy relationships, you should be able to talk about this openly and come to a consensus.

However, if you are unable to talk about this and your partner still shows you that you are last priority, you need to reassess who you are with.

How often do you and your partner go on date nights?
What do your date nights usually look like?

_____

_____

_____

_____

_____

_____

_____

_____

_____

_____

_____

In what ways does your partner show you (or not show
you) that you are a priority?

_____

_____

_____

_____

_____

_____

_____

_____

_____

_____

_____

_____

How are you showing your partner that they are a priority?

_____

_____

_____

_____

_____

_____

_____

_____

Write down the balance of effort in your relationship – who gives more, who takes more, and why you think this is.

_____

_____

_____

_____

_____

_____

_____

_____

Healthy relationships require a lot of work, but they aren't supposed to be exhausting. Maintaining a good relationship can feel wonderful with the right person. If you love yourself, heal prior wounds you may have brought into the relationship, and keep these universal truths in mind about healthy relationships, you equip yourself with everything you need to truly be in a happy relationship. If your partner cannot or will not try, you may need to rethink this relationship.

Chapter 3
How to quickly identify toxic people

A lthough it is difficult to spot a toxic person in the first few meetings, there are some quick tell-tale signs you can remember. If you are a person who has a tendency to fall for toxic people, then it is probably because you need some practice on how to identify them early on so that you do not get emotionally invested too quickly. Ordinarily, you may not be able to recognize the red flags this person is waving, or may choose to give them the benefit of the doubt. However, each time you do this, you are becoming more invested in a relationship with a toxic person and it can be devastatingly painful to get out of it.

After going through strenuous relationships with difficult people, it can feel like an uphill battle to trust somebody new again. It is understandable; it takes a lot to trust another person out there not to hurt you again, but it is important to remember that not every person is toxic, and that you can save yourself from a lot of pain if you are able to recognize the toxic ones quickly. Sometimes it can be tough to identify a toxic person in the beginning stage of the relationship, so learning these traits can help you steer clear of toxicity the next time you see it in a person:

1. *Everything is about them*

They will make everything about themselves - whether it is during a general conversation, your accomplishments, your date-night plans - everything will revolve around what they want and need, without taking your needs into consideration. It is a narcissistic personality trait and can be extremely frustrating to deal with in a relationship. Every single thing is done according to their convenience, and if not, they do not hold back on letting you know that they are not happy about it. It would feel as though the show is all about them and you would be stuck reluctantly cheering in the audience. Constantly. You would never be in the spotlight.

It can be very off-putting and nauseating to constantly feel as though the relationship solely caters to their needs. Feeling invisible can cause feelings of resentment and sadness, and having these feelings usually does not bode well for a relationship. If you have a gut feeling that the person you are dating has narcissistic traits, you are probably right.

What do you and your partner usually talk about? How much of your conversations revolve around them?

_____

_____

_____

_____

_____

_____

_____

_____

How often do they ask about you? When was the last time they did?

_____

_____

_____

_____

_____

_____

_____

_____

Do you think they care about you? Why/Why not? Use your instincts to answer.

_____

_____

_____

_____

_____

_____

_____

_____

_____

_____

_____

_____

2. They do not recognize their own insecurities and emotional scars

We all have our own insecurities and emotional baggage that we carry around. Being imperfect is a normal part of the human life cycle and is actually necessary in order for us to learn and grow. A non-toxic person would be able to recognize their own emotional scars and insecurities, and accept that they are a part of who they are. Furthermore, they would introspect and learn how their emotional scars affect their life and the lives of others, and therefore attempt to heal their wounds so they can live a happier and healthier life.

A toxic and unhealthy person, on the other hand, would not recognize their emotional wounds, and if they did, they would not be willing to work on healing them. Without them taking responsibility for their internal struggles, they will either project those onto you and blame you, or leave you. If they are unable to reflect and see where their insecurities have played a part in their bad behaviour, then they will be defensive and will not attempt to see where you are coming from. To them, they are perfect and you are always at fault.

Do you know what your partner's emotional wounds and insecurities are? Write down what you think they are.

_____

_____

_____

_____

_____

_____

_____

_____

_____

Do they know what their emotional wounds and insecurities are? Explain why you think they may or may not know.

_____

_____

_____

_____

_____

_____

_____

_____

_____

_____

3. They will usually blame their ex

Not every relationship will be a dream come true, and some may even end on unsavory terms. While it is preferable to end relationships amicably, this may not be the case for everybody and that is just a part of life that we have to accept. After we go through our grieving process, healthy individuals usually move on and try to let go of the resentment they hold from their past relationships.

A toxic individual will not be able to let go and will blame their ex for everything that went wrong in the relationship, and maybe in their life too. Of course, their ex might have actually caused some issues in the relationship, but it is never only one person's fault. It takes two to tango. Since the toxic person believes they can do no wrong, they will not take responsibility for the part they played in that relationship. As a narcissistic toxic person, they will genuinely believe that they were innocent and that their ex was the sole reason for the relationship's downfall – there is no room for compromise or introspection. If they do, by chance, recognize what part they played in the relationship, you probably still will not see them do any self-work to grow and rectify those traits in themselves.

Does your partner often talk about their ex(es)? When do they usually bring them up?

_____

_____

_____

_____

_____

_____

_____

_____

_____

_____

What does your partner usually say about their ex(es)?

_____
_____
_____
_____
_____
_____
_____
_____
_____
_____
_____
_____
_____
_____

How do they respond when you bring up their past relationships?

_____
_____
_____
_____
_____
_____
_____
_____
_____
_____
_____
_____
_____
_____

4. They are inconsistent

Inconsistency is arguably one of the most emotionally taxing parts of being in a relationship with a toxic person. The hot and cold of the relationship takes a toll on you and can leave you feeling disheartened and unimportant. Examples of inconsistency can include them saying one thing but doing another, disappearing on you for a few days, having erratic mood swings, being super romantic and then apathetic, and so on.

The problem with inconsistency is that the unpredictability of your partner frustrates you, but it also entices you to hold on to them, as you do see glimpses of the good times and you hope that they may change for the better one day. Sadly, a leopard cannot change its spots. By staying with them throughout their unpredictability, you are actually reinforcing their inconsistency, because they will see that no matter what they do, you will never leave them. Thus, they take advantage of it.

It is important to stand up for yourself when you notice their inconsistencies and call them out on it. Show them that they cannot walk all over you and you deserve some stability. You need to set a high standard and be confident enough to say to yourself "I'm amazing, and I deserve better." If they truly love you and are willing to work on themselves, they will adhere to your standards.

What do you think your partner wants from life? Do you think they know what they want from life?

_____
_____
_____
_____
_____
_____

Have they been inconsistent with you? Write down some examples.

_____

_____

_____

_____

_____

_____

_____

_____

_____

_____

_____

_____

5. *They engage in verbal, substance, physical or sexual abuse*

It is common knowledge that any type of abuse is a big no-no, but yet this still goes unchecked. If your partner has any of these abusive tendencies, then they are definitely a toxic person. Substance abuse can be tough, as addiction is a disease and can cause a lot of problems in a relationship. A person who is willing to change will do everything they can to try and get better, however a toxic person will most likely justify their substance abuse. Verbal, physical and sexual abuse are never acceptable and if your partner has any of these abusive tendencies, this is your cue to leave. No one deserves the scars from any of these kinds of abuse.

Being abusive shows that they cannot react to situations rationally and that they do not handle confrontation well at all. In these situations, you need to ask yourself – can you handle this? Chances are the answer is no. It will become too emotionally draining for you at some point and you will end up losing yourself in the relationship, trying to change them. Hoping for a miracle. A toxic person thinks they are perfect and that their behaviour is excusable because they are the victims in life. The sad news is that unless some supernatural force performs some miracle, they are most likely not going to change. This is when you leave. Being abused can traumatize you for a very long time and affect multiple spheres of your life, so it is essential to walk away from your partner if you are a victim of these types of abuse.

Does your partner have any of the abusive behaviours mentioned above? Explain in detail.

_____

_____

_____

_____

_____

_____

_____

_____

_____

_____

_____

_____

_____

_____

_____

_____

You cannot control how toxic your partner is, but you can control how much love and respect you have for yourself. You can control how much you choose to tolerate and who you allow to stay in your life. The minute you recognize how much better you deserve, you will want to walk away from all the toxicity and you will start attracting genuine, amazing and caring people into your life. It all starts from within.

Part 2
Recognizing Abuse

T his section of the workbook digs deeper into what emotional abuse looks like in daily life and why abusers target certain people. In addition to the abusive tactics you learned in Part 1, this section will reveal more warning signs to look out for when you suspect your current partner or potential new partner is abusive.

You will also learn how to be more self-aware and identify traits about yourself that may be tolerating this type of abuse. Many times, you may not realize how your reactions or words can further instigate your partner to abuse you more. Not to say that it is your fault, but abusers know how to feed off of certain personality traits and take advantage of you, without you even realizing. You will not be able to control your partner's behaviour, but you can definitely change yours based on the knowledge you gain and the exercises you do in this workbook.

The aim of Part 2 is to help you recognize abuse so that you are able to remove yourself out of the equation and realize that their need to abuse is not about you, it is solely about your partner and their emotional wounds. By the end of this section, you will have the sharp skills needed to protect yourself from being dragged into the abusive cycle and get yourself out of it more effectively than before.

Let's get started.

Chapter 4
Why empaths attract toxic people

E mpaths are remarkable. They are highly intuitive, emotionally intelligent and have an exceptional understanding of people's vibes, energies and emotions right off the bat. Empaths are extremely loyal and caring – they prefer to see the good in people and there is no limit to how much an empath can deeply love someone. They feed off of the energy of their surroundings and can bring their own energy to the same level of another person's energy. Empaths are selfless and extremely generous. They are the human version of a rainbow – they will take the sun and the rain from a person, and turn it into something beautiful based on what your needs are. Empaths will always make people feel heard and understood, because they have an innate ability to understand emotions outside of their own perspective. They can be there for anybody and will be there to listen, sometimes a little too often that they may give more than they get. People feel right at home when they talk to an empath.

If you are an empath, you are probably all too familiar with these character traits and people love you for them. You get along with most people and everybody seems to love being around you.

How do you usually prefer to see people? What is your outlook on life and other people?

_____

_____

_____

_____

_____

_____

_____

Write down some instances where you were able to instantly tell what someone else was feeling.

_____

_____

_____

_____

_____

_____

_____

_____

_____

_____

_____

_____

_____

Describe the extent to how emotional you can get.

_____

_____

_____

_____

_____

_____

_____

_____

_____

_____

_____

_____

Do you feel as though you give more than you take? Write down examples of when you think you gave too much.

The biggest drawback of being an empath? There is a tendency to also attract toxic people. You might have noticed this at some point in your life and wondered, "why?!"

The answer is – because you care about people TOO much. You can understand why people act in a certain way and justify their behaviour with some sort of emotional reasoning. As a result, you are able to do this with a toxic person or an emotional abuser as well.

You consider what they have been through in life, or what they are currently feeling, and you empathize to the extent where you excuse their toxic behaviour and allow it to happen due to their circumstances or emotional wounds.

You will probably forgive their bad behaviour and give them the benefit of doubt in some form or another because they may have had a difficult childhood or gone through a particularly toxic break-up. Due to this, unfortunately, an empath becomes the perfect target for an emotional abuser because they know that the empath will justify their behaviour and they can get away with anything.

An emotional abuser is not nearly (if at all) as empathetic as empaths, as they are mostly concerned about themselves. However, they are usually not capable of giving themselves what they need, and so they seek out people (usually empaths) to fulfill their needs – whether it be validation, financial security, sense of power, and so on.

The issue with being an empath is that it is in your nature to give selflessly. While this is a beautiful character trait to have, it can be abused by toxic people. Thus, whatever the emotional abuser needs, they know you will give it to them without much hesitation. In some cases, you will not even realize just how much you are giving and how much they are taking. The toxic person can see that you are a genuinely amazing person and takes advantage of that. They know that you will "understand" and give into what they want.

In addition to being extremely empathetic, add in codependency, and this is a disastrous recipe for an emotionally abusive relationship. Being codependent means you have less self-love for yourself than the norm, and that pushes you to crave love from others. You are dependent on someone else to make you feel validated. It is not easy to blindly love yourself – it takes work – but if you do not try, then you will continue to seek love from other people, even if those people are not good for you. You will expect your partner to constantly reassure you and when they are unable to, you will be left feeling empty.

It is devastating to experience abuse by the person you love the most. But that is the exact problem – you love your partner the most, not yourself, and since you are afraid of being alone, you tolerate their abuse. You could be extremely codependent that if your partner attacked your character, you would probably start believing them.

If your friend came to you feeling insecure about themselves and asked you for reassurance, you would probably tell them all the things that are wonderful about them and tell them they were crazy to not see all these beautiful qualities within them. If you can do that for someone else, why not do it for yourself? The more you love and reassure yourself, the less emotionally dependent you will be on your partner, and the less you will tolerate their abuse. Their hurtful words and actions will not be welcome in your life.

With toxic people in particular, because you crave love from external sources, you will justify their bad behaviour and forgive them, mainly because you do not want to lose them. You will go out of your way to make sure they stick around, because being lonely terrifies you. Your empathetic nature will constantly empathize with the abuser and as a result, you will excuse their behaviour and cater to their wounds, instead of yours.

This codependency signals to the abuser that there are no consequences to their actions and that they can continue to treat you in whatever way they please. They will know that they can show you their true colours and that you will forgive them.

They can also shower you with love and affection and give you what you need, so that you have something to hold on to. They know that you will constantly crave that expression of love and will hope for them to change for the better. This hope for them to change is what makes you stick around and fulfill their every need. For every abusive tactic they throw at you, you might be forgiving them because you remind yourself of those flowers that they got you last week, or the meal they cooked for you, or the loving things they said to you last month. The abuse somehow gets replaced with the infrequent acts of love. However, it is important to remember that at some point, they will hurt you and the cycle will start again.

Describe a few instances when your partner treated you badly and you forgave them.

_____

_____

_____

_____

_____

_____

_____

_____

_____

_____

_____

_____

_____

_____

_____

_____

_____

_____

_____

_____

_____

_____

For each situation you recounted above, why did you for-give them? How did you justify their behaviour?

_____

_____

_____

_____

_____

_____

_____

_____

_____

_____

_____

_____

How does your partner usually seek your forgiveness?

_____

_____

_____

_____

_____

_____

_____

_____

_____

_____

_____

_____

How long do the "good" episodes usually last before your partner starts being abusive again?

_____

_____

_____

_____

_____

_____

_____

_____

_____

_____

_____

_____

How do empaths stop attracting toxic people?

In order to stop attracting toxic people, the first step is to recognize that you are an empath. Observe the way you interact with people and your thought processes when they behave in certain ways. Are you more likely to forgive easily? Do you tend to understand what people are going through? Do you justify people's behaviours based on their circumstances? Being an empath means also having the ability to be introspective, so use this quality to reflect on what behavioural patterns you exhibit as an empath.

Once you are familiar with how you think, feel, and act, educate yourself on what emotional abuse and narcissism look like. It is easy to promise yourself that you are not going to let this happen to you again, but without knowing the signs of these types of behaviours, it can be difficult for you to identify them, take action, and put a stop to them. Read up on what the warning signs are for emotional abuse and narcissism, so that you are better equipped to know when someone is crossing the line. Educating yourself will not be your holy grail to stop emotional abuse, but it is also a big step toward being able to cut toxic people from your life.

Simultaneously, make self-love a priority. The tolerance for abuse comes from a lack of love for oneself and a fear of being alone. Do one thing that makes you feel genuinely happy and fulfilled every day. Even if it is for a short amount of time or if it is an extremely simple activity – allocating time to treat yourself like the most important person in the world will help you realize how amazing and wonderful you really are. You will start to feel more whole as a person and you will start to see other aspects of your life apart from your partner can make you feel great! You can even make lists of things you love about yourself and read them every day to remind yourself of how lovable you are. Do whatever you think it will take to make you see your worth. You will start to believe you deserve better and as a result, you will commit to enforcing your boundaries. You can empathize with other people and still draw the line when you feel uncomfortable. Shower yourself with love to the point where you do not feel empty and crave love from anybody else – you will know just how amazing you are. Think of it as though you are dating yourself – spend time with yourself, get yourself gifts, take yourself on dates, and do things you love. Get to know yourself on a deeper level. Pretty soon, you will start to feel whole and complete from within.

What are some activities you can do for yourself regularly to feel more fulfilled?

_____

_____

_____

_____

_____

_____

Make a list of qualities you love about yourself.

As you maintain the combination of loving yourself and educating yourself on the warning signs of toxicity, you will be able to easily understand where things are going wrong in your relationship and what is not acceptable. Additionally, familiarizing yourself on what healthy relationships look like is also crucial. If you think you have been surrounded with unhealthy relationships and are unaware of what healthy relationships look like, you could do some research on that, just so that you know what some healthy benchmarks are. Based on that, you would know how far off your relationship is to a healthy one.

Abusive relationships can leave you with almost no capability to trust, and that is okay. It is understandable that you would be hesitant to trust somebody in your first few meetings. Healthy dating is not about falling in love and living happily ever after right off the bat. It is about getting to know the other person through logic and reasoning. The more you learn about the other person, the better you are able to accurately judge whether they are a suitable fit for you. Love and trust are built as you go along and emerge later in the relationship, so it is important not to rush the process. Otherwise, you may be too emotionally invested in the very beginning and if you realize along the way that you both are not compatible, it can be extremely painful to let go, especially if you have codependency issues.

Have faith in the fact that you are strong enough to know your worth and give yourself the best. Once you start truly believing that, you will be able to set boundaries and stop attracting toxic people. Your self-sufficiency will ultimately attract similarly amazing people into your life.

Do you think you are codependent? Why/why not?

_____

_____

_____

_____

_____

_____

_____

_____

_____

_____

_____

_____

Write down some examples of when you forgave toxic be-
haviour out of fear of losing your partner.

_____

_____

_____

_____

_____

_____

_____

_____

_____

_____

_____

_____

_____

Chapter 5
Warning signs of emotional abuse

A s mentioned in Chapter 1, there are several ways in which emotional abusers dominate their partner's lives. The abuser usually exhibits these dominating traits later in the relationship, once their partner is emotionally entrenched in the relationship. Since they only reveal their true colours when you are already deeply invested in the relationship, it is difficult to see your partner for who they truly are early on. In the beginning of the relationship, the abuser is charming and romantic. They shower you with attention, affection and flattery. The relationship is still in its honeymoon phase and you constantly feel its passion – your partner is the reason you smile the minute you wake up in the morning. Human beings, women in particular, crave the romantic attention and grand gestures that we see in movies, and when an abuser shows us that sort of attention, it is easy to fall head over heels in love, despite the red flags that appear along the way. The abuser makes you feel wanted, important and loved – they gain your trust quickly enough so that when the abusive behaviour becomes more evident, you are already in too deep.

Luckily, there are quite a number of tell-tale signs you can look out for, even at the start of the relationship, to determine whether the person you are dating is an emotional abuser:

1. *Love bombing*

Love bombing is exactly what it sounds like – your partner drops these extravagantly massive love bombs on you in order to win you over. This can be in the form of excessive texting, calling, gift-giving, flirting, date-nights, and so on. If you grew up watching fairytales about how the princess and the prince live happily ever after, the love bombing stage will look extremely similar to those fairytales. It feels perfect – you start to think this person is your soulmate and that life cannot get any better than this.

Of course, in the honeymoon phase of the relationship, everything feels exciting and you both cannot seem to get enough of each other. The excitement and passion are normal and actually needed while getting to know somebody. However, if the attention and affection start to feel too extravagant, that is a red flag. Your partner would most likely be love bombing you to ensure that you fall head over heels in love with them and trust them, that way they know they have a hold on you for the rest of the relationship.

Has your partner excessively love bombed you? Describe a few episodes.

_____
_____
_____
_____
_____
_____
_____
_____
_____
_____
_____
_____
_____
_____
_____
_____
_____

2. They have a sense of superiority and criticize you

There is a sort of charm in a person who is confident and knows their worth. When we look for a partner, we consider people who know what they want in life and are confident with themselves to be more attractive. However, there is a fine line between confidence and arrogance. Emotional abusers have a sense of superiority that stems from insecurity. They seek external praise and validation, and if they do not receive that, they project themselves to be superior as a way of masking their insecurities.

One of the ways in which emotional abusers claim their superiority is by criticizing others, especially their partner. A person who exhibits high traits of arrogance has a tendency to belittle others and show that their way of life is the "right way" over that of anybody else's. It gives them the satisfaction to know that they are "better" than everyone else and they make sure everybody knows it. Healthy people have no reason to belittle others, even if they have a vast amount of life experience and knowledge.

Abusive people rarely see any flaws within them, so they do not see any reason to work on themselves and grow. However, they very easily notice flaws in other people and take every chance to point those out to undervalue the person. With their partners in particular, they highlight their superiority through criticism as a way of showing their partner that they are "the best they can ever get" and that they embody the ideal partner anybody would yearn to have. If you face this with your partner, try not to take their criticism and superiority complex as the truth, as it is all a manifestation of their avoidance to introspect. To them, it is easier to criticize others than to criticize themselves.

Has your partner ever acted superior to you and criticized you? Write down a few examples.

_____

_____

_____

_____

_____

_____

_____

_____

_____

_____

_____

_____

_____

_____

_____

_____

_____

_____

_____

_____

_____

_____

_____

_____

_____

_____

_____

_____

_____

_____

_____

3. The relationship is moving too fast

The human species, at some point for the most part, seeks companionship and wants to end up with someone special to spend the rest of their life with.

They crave that happily ever after and seek partners who are willing to commit. While this is a goal that many people wish to achieve, emotional abusers show their potential partners that they are willing to commit a little too quickly.

They do this by demanding you spend most, if not all, of your time with them, give them all of your attention, and announce to the world that you are exclusively committed to them.

When they push for this commitment too quick, it can lead you to feel uncomfortable but also relieved that there are people out there who want to commit (because let's face it, a lot of people nowadays are commitment-phobes).

The flip side to this though, is that the reason the emotional abuser is pushing you to commit to them so soon is so that they can isolate you from your closest circle.

They need your constant attention and validation; thus, they aim to remove you from your social network so that you can give them all your time and energy.

If you feel as though your relationship is moving too fast for comfort, call your partner out on it. If they realize and accept this, then you may be in the clear. However, if they try to justify their isolating you and do not take the conversation well, then there is a pretty good chance you are dealing with an emotional abuser.

Write down some instances when you felt as though your partner was pushing you to commit too quickly.

_____

_____

_____

_____

_____

_____

_____

_____

_____

_____

Write down some episodes of when your partner isolated you from your friends and family.

_____

_____

_____

_____

_____

_____

_____

_____

_____

_____

_____

_____

4. They dominate your life

As mentioned earlier, emotional abusers have this need to control and dictate your life. It is the biggest motivation that drives most of their behaviour and it is important to look out for this particular trait. Many times, you will feel as though your partner is treating you like a 5-year-old and does not allow you to live your life with autonomy. They may insinuate that your dreams and aspirations are "pathetic" and may de-motivate you from achieving your goals.

A common side effect from this type of life domination is that you can get so used to them dictating how you should live your life on their terms, that even when you do have the chance to act autonomously, you may still find yourself consulting them to help you make a decision. You allow them to do so because you do not want to lose them and they have conditioned you to believe that "they know better".

The more you allow them to dominate you, the harder it is for you to break free and live life on your own terms. One reason is because your partner can react extremely poorly to this sudden desire to make your own decisions. If they see you slipping away from their grasp, their insecurities will push them to manipulate you so that you cannot drift away. Another reason it is difficult to break free from an abusive partner is that you may not know how to live after being with them for so long. You may not trust your own instincts and might constantly rely on their advice.

By allowing them to control your life, you are feeding their superiority complex, as they now will believe that they truly do know everything, and that other people's way of living is completely wrong.

If you think you have given too much power to your partner, there are ways to try and regain control over your life, which will be explained in the upcoming chapters.

In what ways has your partner tried to dominate you and control your life?

_____

_____

_____

_____

_____

_____

_____

_____

_____

_____

_____

_____

_____

_____

_____

5. *They obsess over your social media activity*

Social media has integrated into our daily lives to an extent where it has become an integral part of how we communicate with the world. For most of us, it is part of our routine to check social media, post any updates on our lives and keep in touch with our friends. A healthy partner would most likely understand that this is what you are using social media for and that it is just a way to keep in touch with your social network.

However, if your partner obsesses over how much time you spend on social media, who you message, whose posts you like and comment on, and who you follow, this behaviour points towards them having major jealousy issues. They would want you to devote most of your attention to them, no one else (even if it is over a social media app). They will find opportunities to equate you giving someone else attention on social media to you not loving them enough. This kind of jealousy can be toxic for your relationship, as you will start to feel you do not have freedom to do as you please online as well as offline.

What is tricky here is you will want to reassure them because you care for them, and because you may be codependent, you will continuously adhere to their restrictions because you do not want to lose them. The more you give in to their jealous demands, the more time they will carve out of your life. It could come to a point where you may have lost touch with your friends, family, career and aspirations because you gave in to your partner's insecurities each and every time.

Write down the times when your partner has been jealous or gotten upset over your social media usage.

_____
_____
_____
_____
_____
_____
_____
_____
_____
_____
_____
_____
_____
_____
_____

6. *They are hypersensitive and get jealous easily*

As mentioned in the previous point about social media activity, an emotional abuser tends to overreact to you giving other people attention, even if it is a tiny amount of attention on social media. This applies to any sort of attention in the real world as well. Your partner will get jealous over someone who is trying to talk to you, or sends you a message, or they could even get jealous when you try to hang out with someone of the same sex as them.

A little jealousy once in a while is completely okay – it shows that the person cares for you and does not want to lose you. A little sprinkle of jealousy is okay as long as they understand that they are the one you chose to be with and that they can trust you. Emotional abusers, on the other hand, get jealous of little things and do not trust your word. If you do not agree with them, they get hypersensitive and it leads to a huge conflict. This behaviour stems from their own insecurities and low self-esteem. Since they are not confident about themselves, they view anybody you interact with as a threat.

Dealing with an emotionally abusive partner's jealousy can be exhausting. They perceive your reassurance as insults sometimes and get more paranoid about who you interact with. Even if you tell them that they are the most important person in the world, they can somehow manage to spin that around to make it sound like you said you do not care about them.

They want you to be accessible to them at all times and they should be the "only" person on your mind. You may have tried to express to them how smothered this makes you feel, but somehow, they are able to justify their mistrust and get you to agree to reduce the amount you interact with whomever they perceive as a threat. The more you do this, the more people you will lose touch with. You will be giving them more authority over your life, and that is painful.

When has your partner gotten jealous? How have you both dealt with the jealousy?

---

7. *They always blame you*

As you may know, emotional abusers rarely take responsibility for anything they have done wrong. They blame their issues on the world and never look within themselves to see if they are the ones who caused the issues, since they believe they have no faults. If anybody does try to blame them for what they have done, this does not sit well with them, at all. They start insulting the other person and start blaming them for everything that has gone wrong, while insisting that the other person agrees with them.

Emotional abusers take life way too seriously and tend to play the victim card. Everything has always "happened to them" and they are usually able to find a reason to complain about it. With any aspect of their life, whether it is regarding their career, education, relationship or family, they take responsibility for the good things that happened, but never for the issues they might have caused. They have not learned how to take responsibility for the actions in their life and, as a result, have rarely had to deal with any consequences either.

Has your partner ever blamed how they feel or their issues on you? Write down some examples.

_____

_____

_____

_____

_____

_____

_____

_____

_____

_____

_____

8. They degrade and humiliate you

Emotional abusers feel superior by belittling and humiliating you. They project their insecurities onto you and insult you so that they can slap a band-aid on their issues and feel superior for that moment. This can happen in the form of insults, sarcasm and invalidation. The hurtful words that they use can really shatter your confidence and make you believe you are not good enough.

When your partner degrades you in public, it signifies a lack of respect for you as a person. Humiliation can be traumatizing and an emotional abuser does not consider the pain it causes you. Degrading you in front of other people can lower your self-esteem, which ultimately can make you more emotionally vulnerable for love and validation, which you would expect to come from your partner. Even though they are the one that made you feel humiliated, the emotions you feel make you seek their reassurance to feel validated again. This is the vicious cycle that many codependent victims have a tough time getting out of.

If your partner has humiliated you in front of other people and have invalidated your confrontation to them, then you are probably dealing with an emotionally abusive partner who does not respect you or your feelings.

Were there any times when your partner humiliated you in public? Write down those episodes.

_____

_____

_____

_____

_____

_____

_____

_____

_____

_____

9. They neglect or ignore you

A healthy partner will never neglect or ignore you. The relationship will be fruitful and both partners' needs will be addressed to the best of the couple's abilities. An emotionally abusive partner, on the other hand, will solely think about their needs and neglect those of their partner. The relationship will revolve mostly around the abusive partner and they will fail to recognize what they are not bringing to the table for you. You may start to resent them and feel as though your needs do not matter.

The abusive partner can take it one step further and blatantly ignore you. If you bring up a topic that your partner does not want to talk about, or if they feel as though you are "attacking" them, they will punish you by stonewalling. Stonewalling is when the other person completely shuts down and does not respond to you – they withhold affection and attention. Some people use stonewalling due to their incapability of processing emotions, but some (such as abusers) use it as a form of punishment.

You could be asking them questions right to their face and they will blatantly ignore you. They avoid making eye contact, their body language is dismissive, they become "busy" when you need to talk to them, and if they do speak it is usually to defend themselves or invalidate your concerns. Ultimately, you start to feel extremely frustrated because you do not feel heard. They know this gets to you; they also know that you will end up agreeing to meet their needs in an attempt to win their affection back. While stonewalling may be a coping mechanism for your partner, it is considered abuse as it causes significant emotional turmoil within you.

Being neglected and ignored can be devastating and is a major sign of inconsistency in the relationship. One minute your partner could be speaking with you about something completely casual, and the next minute they could be ignoring you because you disagreed with them.

Does your partner ignore you or neglect your needs? Give a few examples.

_____
_____
_____
_____
_____
_____
_____
_____
_____
_____

10. They are codependent

In most emotionally abusive relationships, the non-abusive partner is codependent on the abusive partner, which is why codependent personalities are usually the abuser's target. However, emotionally abusive partners are just as codependent on their partners. They need to have power over you in order to feel complete. They do not respect your boundaries and they treat you as though you are an extension of them. Most of the time, they do not acknowledge your individuality and project their personality onto you. They may expect you to think like them or have the same aspirations and opinions as them, and if you do not, this upsets them.

By them thinking of you both as one entity, you end up feeling suffocated in the relationship and feel as though you are dating a dictator. When you try to bring up this issue, they could justify their behaviour by saying that they know what is best for you and that you should listen to them.

When you have been dating an emotional abuser for so long and you love them, it can be difficult to accept that your partner may not always have your best interest at heart, and only have theirs in mind. It is important to establish your individuality early on in the relationship, so that it becomes tough for them to mesh their personality with yours. One of the biggest injustices you could do is lose your sense of self.

Has your partner told you what is best for you and expected you to live life like they do? Write down some examples of when this has happened.

_____

_____

_____

_____

_____

_____

_____

_____

_____

_____

_____

_____

_____

_____

11. They have unrealistic expectations

If your partner is emotionally abusive, chances are they have highly unrealistic expectations. It is human nature to have certain expectations from life and people, but healthy people are able to manage their expectations so that their partner does not feel pressured or inadequate. Emotionally abusive partners, on the other hand, expect you to be a certain way for them and if you are anything "less", they lash out or insult you. These expectations can be based on the gender roles they have in mind, the way you dress, the way you manage your finances – basically the way you live your life. Their emotional reactions stem from them not being able to accept you for who you are, and as a result, they react from a place of disappointment. This is not healthy. Emotionally healthy relationships entail two people accepting each other for who they truly are at the core.

Again, the abuser wants to control you and treats you like an extension of themselves, and so if you are not living up to what they expect from you, they are going to be hard on you. Their superiority complex makes them believe they know best and that you should follow what they say if you are to be worthy of being their partner.

Speak up if you are uncomfortable with any of these expectations, as you are still your own person and you have every right to live your life the way you want to.

What does your partner expect of you? Are you comfortable with these expectations?

_____

_____

_____

_____

_____

_____

_____

_____

_____

_____

_____

_____

_____

_____

_____

_____

_____

_____

_____

_____

12. They isolate you from your social network

Since emotional abusers want all your time and energy to be focused solely on them, they make you feel guilty about giving any attention to your close friends and family. They seek validation from you and if they observe you giving any sort of validation to another person, they start to feel jealous. So, they manipulate you to distance yourself from anyone that distracts you from your relationship with them. They can do this by guilt-tripping you into cancelling plans with friends, ignoring phone calls from family, or even by blaming you for them feeling lonely. Before you know it, you have isolated yourself from your closest friends and family. Your partner can also get you to do this by shaming you, criticizing your social network and making you feel guilty that you do not give your partner "as much attention" as they give you. They can be very unwelcoming of your network and can even make them feel uncomfortable to the extent that your network does not want to interact with you or your partner any more.

If you still want to hang out with your friends, your partner will most likely formulate false conclusions as to why you prefer to hang out with them. This can lead to nasty fights and can make you feel obliged to constantly give them your attention, even when you are just trying to have a fun night out with your friends. When you are hanging out with your friends, you will probably be conditioned to feel guilty for doing so, because your partner would have burned it into your brain at this point. Try to identify when this happens and remind yourself that you are totally allowed to have a life outside of your relationship. In fact, it is necessary.

Has your partner made you feel guilty for hanging out with your friends or family? Write down some instances.

_____
_____
_____
_____
_____
_____
_____
_____
_____
_____
_____

Have they made you lose touch with anybody? How and why?

_____
_____
_____
_____
_____
_____
_____
_____
_____
_____
_____
_____
_____
_____

13. *They treat others poorly*

This is common knowledge, but a big warning sign of an emotional abuser is that they treat other people poorly. If they have a tendency to blame strangers when they bump into them on the street, or lash out at the host of a restaurant for keeping them waiting too long, there is a good chance they have an abusive personality. They feel entitled to have things done their way and their egos tell them that they are the most important person in the world. If they suspect someone is defying that belief of theirs, they treat them poorly.

A healthy person would give other people the benefit of the doubt and let it go. An emotionally abusive person will take the event too personally and make the other person feel guilty until they apologize. The abuser will most likely never apologize for their behaviour, but expects others to apologize to feed the abuser's ego.

A healthy relationship entails your partner respecting you as well as others, and being able to recognize when they have crossed the line. If you notice that your partner disrespects other people, and they get defensive when you bring up their behaviour with them, then that is a major red flag.

How does your partner treat other people? Can you recall some times when your partner treated other people poorly?

_____

_____

_____

_____

_____

_____

_____

_____

_____

_____

_____

_____

_____

_____

_____

_____

_____

_____

_____

_____

Of course, nobody is perfect and everyone may exhibit some of these signs at some point to some degree. However, if you observe your partner exhibiting most of these signs very often, your partner is an emotional abuser.

Chapter 6
Trauma Bonding: Why you are unable to leave a toxic relationship

We meet lots of different people as we go on with our lives. With each person we meet, we share experiences with them and form a connection. The more we get to know the person, the deeper the connection becomes and we ultimately form a deep bond with them. We all have multiple bonds we share with people and, most of the time, these are bonds that we have chosen to make with those specific people.

Since we bond with different kinds of people, we may find ourselves bonding with a toxic person at some point in our life too. This may have happened to you, wherein you find yourself establishing a connection with someone who did not seem to be toxic at first, but over time showed you their true colours and turned out to be quite emotionally abusive. However, due to the connection you now share with them, you have created a bond filled with shared experiences, shared lives, maybe even shared children and homes.

Trauma bonding is when the bond you have formed with an emotionally abusive person builds trauma for you over a long period of time, possibly throughout the relationship. Every gaslighting episode, manipulation, insult and so on, adds to the bank of trauma you incur from the bond. Logically, it would make sense to leave the person you are trauma bonding with, so that you can be free of the abuse. Unfortunately, it is not always easy, and that is understandable. You are a human with emotions. When you have formed a deep bond with your partner, you do have love for them and it can be heart-wrenching to pull away from that, especially since there may have been some good times in the relationship as well. If you have children with this person, then that makes it even harder to leave them.

Ultimately, you feel stuck in a cycle in which you know this person is toxic for you and you need to leave, but you are not able to. Why does trauma bonding happen? It usually forms based on what you think a normal relationship looks like, which is molded in your childhood. If you grew up seeing your parents exhibiting an emotionally abusive relationship, this was the primary relationship model that stuck in your mind and you grew up believing that this was what relationships should look like. If you were not constantly exposed to healthy relationships, you would not have known what they look like. As a result, your model for relationships was based on the emotionally abusive relationship between your parents or your primary caretakers.

As you got older, you started to notice what emotionally abusive behaviour looked like in your own relationships, however you built such a strong tolerance for it as a child when viewing your parents' relationship, that you convinced yourself that this was just a part of being in love. If we are not healthy within ourselves, then we tend to bond with people who are emotionally abusive, narcissistic or toxic, because we have not set those standards of what we want our healthy relationship to look like. It is the wounds within ourselves that dictate what kind of relationship we attract, and if it is with a toxic person, chances are we will trauma bond and it will be extremely difficult for us to leave.

Trauma bonding is like an addiction. Your mind and body are essentially addicted to this person, and when you try to quit the addiction, you experience withdrawal symptoms. You could even fear the withdrawal symptoms before they set in. Like a drug, you would probably go through a roller coaster of emotions and sensations with this person, you would experience all the highs and lows. However, what keeps you addicted are the high moments – the times when your partner showed you the best version of themselves; the times when they love bombed you; the times when you actually thought they could be an amazing partner and could permanently change for the better. The thought of leaving them and the pain that comes with it makes you want to stay with them even more, because you probably do not want to go through those withdrawal symptoms.

So, how do we know if we are trauma bonding? What are the symptoms?

1. Feeling stuck

First and foremost, you feel stuck in a never-ending cycle. Your partner shows you time and time again that they are toxic and you know that you would probably be better off without them, but the bond that you have created with this person prevents you from making that move. Your logical side knows that this person is not good for you and you need to leave, but your emotional side fights back and convinces you that you need to stay out of fear of what the consequences may be if you did leave.

Have you felt stuck in this cycle? Write down some times when you tried to leave but then could not.

_____

_____

_____

_____

_____

_____

_____

_____

_____

_____

_____

_____

_____

_____

_____

_____

_____

2. Your close network notices how different you have become.

Dealing with an emotionally abusive relationship can take its toll on you, and might change the way you perceive life. Your friends and family will notice this about you and tell you that you have changed. They will probably say that you have lost your spark and excitement for life, or that you look worn out and that they are worried about you. Some may even know you have changed and will question why you are still with your partner.

Has anybody told you that you have become different because of your relationship? Write down the details.

_____
_____
_____
_____
_____
_____
_____
_____
_____
_____
_____
_____
_____
_____
_____
_____
_____
_____

3. *You still believe that your partner is a good person*

The bond you have formed with your partner is overpowering and can cloud your judgment. After all, the bond has good aspects to it as well. You have seen some amazing qualities your partner has to offer and you have received love and affection from them.

However, this was most likely not consistent and you only saw these great qualities at times. Your logical side knows that they are inconsistent, but your emotional side believes that if they can exhibit good traits sometimes, then there is hope that they will change and be amazing all the time.

Due to your emotional vulnerability, you see the traits you want to see, and not the entire person as a whole.

If you have mastered the art of self-love, you would not mask your judgment with your hopes, you would allow them to show you who they truly are and then you would make your decision on whether you want to continue pursuing the relationship.

It is incredibly difficult to accept this when you have trauma bonded with your partner, especially if you have some emotional wounds you need to heal, but the important thing is to recognize this first.

Write down the good qualities in your partner, and then write down the abusive ones.

Good qualities:

_____

_____

_____

_____

_____

_____

_____

_____

_____

_____

_____

Abusive qualities:

_____

_____

_____

_____

_____

_____

_____

_____

_____

_____

_____

_____

How do we stop trauma bonding?

If you think you are trauma bonding with someone early on, take a step back and reflect on what aspects of the relationship are traumatizing you. What are the unhealthy aspects about this relationship or person that are familiar to you? What has made this bond go from a healthy one to a trauma one? Once you analyze all of this, you can start to distance yourself before you get too emotionally invested.

If you are already in a committed relationship with someone you have trauma bonded with, it can be extremely difficult to let go. Emotions are at play, and it can be tremendously painful to even think about leaving, even though you know it is the right thing to do yourself. How do we make this easy?

1. *Acceptance*

Accept that the relationship is toxic and that your partner is emotionally abusive. Accept that despite the trauma you endure from this relationship, you are probably addicted to this person and have trouble letting go. Acknowledge that this person does have their flaws and they have clearly shown them to you time and time again. Most problems cannot be solved if you are in denial about the nature of your relationship, so remember that acceptance is the first step to dealing with any problem. Once you have accepted that your relationship has emotionally abusive qualities, you can move on to the next step.

2. *Make the choice to be happy*

Once you have accepted that this relationship is making you more miserable than it is giving you peace, make the decision to be happy. That means leaving the relationship. It might be the most painful thing you have ever had to do, and that is understandable. You spent so much of your time and energy with this person while sharing your life and experiences with them. Leaving them requires strength, which you do have within you, you just need to believe that you can access it.

Start asking yourself: What makes me happy? What makes me feel confident? How do I want my life to turn out? By answering these questions, you start to prioritize your happiness and you will not allow anything to get in the way of you loving yourself. It will be a difficult process, but nothing amazing comes without hard work. You will need to grow and learn things about yourself that you may never have known, and this is what will help give you the strength to walk away. The minute you choose to have a happy life, work on yourself to the point where you do not let anything or anyone get in the way of that.

3. *Keep encouraging yourself*

Leaving your partner is a big decision and will be devastating. You are taking a huge step here and it is going to be overwhelming. You will probably start catastrophizing what life may be like once you leave, and that usually happens when you think of the big scary picture. This causes anxiety and, as a result, you find yourself stuck in the cycle again.

In order to break out of the cycle, remember that you are on your way to healing and that healing is a journey. You may relapse, and that is expected – nobody is perfect. You may feel the temptation to reach out to them or may find yourself thinking about them all the time. Give yourself time and credit. You are doing the best you can and it will take you time to get used to life without this person. You will learn how to deal with each painful moment on your own, which will give you strength and happiness you cannot even imagine. Ensure you give yourself an infinite amount of love throughout this process, because you are going to need it and who better to love you than you.

4. *Follow through*

When you do leave your partner, keep reminding yourself that you are doing what is best for your mental health and sanity. You are closing the door on toxicity and opening the door to happiness. Keep going, even when it gets unbearable. Follow through on your commitment to yourself to let go of the addiction to this person and the emotional abuse.

This entire process will show you that you do have what it takes to put yourself first. It will be tough to leave, but once you do, you will realize you have so much strength within you.

Knowing what trauma bonding is and how you can break that bond is a great step toward you attaining your healthier and happier life, and soon enough you might find someone better suited for you.

What was your parents' or primary caretakers' relationship like? Did you notice any emotionally abusive qualities?

_____

_____

_____

_____

_____

_____

_____

_____

_____

_____

As your partner's abuse intensifies, do you find yourself moving away or toward your partner? Write down some instances.

_____

_____

_____

_____

_____

_____

_____

_____

_____

_____

_____

When you are disconnected from your partner, how does that make you feel?

_____

_____

_____

_____

_____

_____

_____

_____

_____

_____

_____

Which abusive qualities have made you want to leave your partner?

_____

_____

_____

_____

_____

_____

_____

_____

_____

_____

_____

_____

Chapter 7
Projection and Emotional Abuse

I n order to recognize when your partner is being emotionally abusive, it is crucial to understand what projection is. Projection is
when someone has a feeling (usually an uncomfortable feeling) and at-
tributes it to another person. Projection is a defense mechanism that
helps the person to avoid confronting the uncomfortable feeling and
shift the negative attention to someone else. For example, if someone
were feeling guilty about not visiting their sick mother and they were
having a conversation with someone else, they would project their guilt
onto that other person in order to make the other person feel guilty, so
that they would be relieved of processing their own guilt. Projection is
not usually intentional – the person may not be aware that they are having this particular feeling for a specific reason, but they know that they
are feeling uncomfortable and so they transfer that feeling to another
person, in the hopes that the discomfort goes away.

The human mind has an interesting way of bringing suppressed
thoughts and emotions to the forefront of our minds. Even if we do not
want to deal with them and we try to push those feelings down as far as
we can, the mind decides to resurface those feelings so that we deal with
them head on. The more we suppress, the more those feelings will push
to break down those barriers we have created, and this can result in
some emotionally, and sometimes physically, destructive consequences. At some point, we do need to face our feelings, even the uncomfortable ones, and process them correctly.

Projection is usually manifested from anger. If someone is projecting
their feelings onto you, it probably feels like they are attacking you and
their tone can be aggressive. The anger comes from the discomfort they
are feeling from a negative emotion. They try to avoid it as much as they
can, but the uncomfortable feeling within them does not completely
disappear, it stays hidden somewhere in the mind. The person does not
know how to process this discomfort, and in turn gets angry and pro-

jects it onto you. Try to notice next time someone gets aggressive or angry with you – what are they actually angry about it? Are they harbouring some insecurities? Do you think they are projecting their own fears onto you? Recognizing projection is the first step to protecting yourself from emotional abuse.

Why does projection happen? It is common for human beings to be scared of their emotions. Why do we get so scared though? Emotions are basically just sensations. We experience them in our minds and in our bodies – maybe through a racing heart, a lump in the throat, tears strolling down our face, or a sick feeling in our stomachs. Challenging emotions make us feel worse than they do better, and we have a tendency to run away from the potential pain. While it is understandable, it is not completely rational, as those emotions are just sensations in the body, they are not life-threatening. Feelings are fleeting sensations that do not last forever; they are temporary. Our egos label them as "negative emotions" and tell us to run far away from them in order to safeguard ourselves. However, it turns out that instead of safeguarding, we are suppressing those feelings and choosing to cope with them in an unhealthy way.

Emotional abusers rarely own up to their feelings and blame other people for their problems. As you can imagine, projection is a very convenient defense mechanism for toxic people. They cannot take responsibility for any challenging emotion that they have, and will end up guilt-tripping or shaming you – they will probably say you are selfish, obsessive, nagging, and so on. They do this because their subconscious is attempting to bring their uncomfortable feelings under the spotlight, but the person's ego is pushing that spotlight onto you so that they do not have to deal with that discomfort. Being able to recognize projection is the first step to dealing with it. If you are not able to identify when someone may be projecting, you will take what they say too personally and start getting defensive. Having low self-confidence adds another layer of you potentially believing what your partner is projecting onto you, and you will start to assume that what they are saying about you is accurate. You will end up tangled in this conversation, feeling horrible, while your partner has just transferred their discomfort onto you and is feeling much better because of it.

It is essential to be able to recognize when they are projecting so that you can take a step back and avoid entangling your self-worth into the conversation. This is why it is so important to build your self-confidence. If you are confident within yourself and you know this person is projecting, you will not take what they say personally and you will know that this is all about them, not you. It will not affect you on a deeper level and you will not get as emotionally invested. It takes practice, but the more you do it, the easier it will be to hold onto yourself when they do project.

Calling out a toxic person when they are projecting may not always bode well for you, as they most likely will still not accept that they are projecting and will continue to insult you. Remember, this is not about you, it is all about them not being able to look at themselves in the mirror and own up to their feelings. Hold yourself together and keep loving yourself throughout the process. You will probably need some validation at that point, which your partner may not be able to give you. So, it is important for you to be able to validate your own self-worth so that no matter what they project, you are emotionally strong.

While projections are usually negative and aggressive in nature, there is also positive projection. Positive projection is when you are feeling insecure about something and you project your wants onto someone else. For example, if you meet someone amazing and you really want it to work out, you might project this want onto them and look at them through filtered glasses. You will not give them a chance to show you who they truly are because you would only make yourself see what you want to see. It would be like going to an art class with an already painted canvas, instead of going with a blank one and allowing people to paint it there, over a period of time. Be careful not to positively project your wants onto your partner if you are seeking only the good traits in them. Remember to look at the whole picture.

Disassociating from projection can be difficult, as our subconscious comes into play and we do not always know when we are projecting. With practice comes perfection and the more you consciously confront your feelings, the less likely you are to project. When dealing with an emotionally abusive partner who is projecting, consistently give yourself love and affection, and remind yourself of your worth. Remind yourself that you know how amazing you are and nobody can take that away from you, no matter what they say. You got this.

Write down some examples of when your partner has projected their feelings onto you.

_____

_____

_____

_____

_____

_____

_____

_____

_____

_____

_____

_____

_____

_____

_____

_____

Have there been times when you believed what your partner was projecting onto you to be true? Write down some examples.

_____

_____

_____

_____

_____

_____

_____

_____

_____

_____

Do you think you engage in positive projection in order to see only the good qualities in your partner? Write down details.

_____

_____

_____

_____

_____

_____

_____

_____

_____

_____

Chapter 8
Cognitive Dissonance

C ognitive dissonance is a psychological concept that applies to lots of situations in our life. Once you understand what it is, you will probably realize just how many times you go through it, especially in an emotionally abusive relationship.

Cognitive dissonance is the mental stress incurred due to a conflict between your belief based on the past, and what you are facing in the present. It happens when your mind has formed opinions on previous situations based on the reality at that time, and now those opinions do not seem to match what is happening in the present moment. Due to this contradiction, your mind struggles to believe what is actually real – the past or the present.

Cognitive dissonance is especially relevant in emotionally abusive relationships, as you struggle to believe what is real about your partner. Their actions may not match their words, or the way they used to be does not match how they act now, and this can throw you off.

Toxic partners are inconsistent and this inconsistency causes you to constantly question which version of your partner is the real one, and when feelings of love are involved, that can further amplify the effects of cognitive dissonance.

We call the beginning stage of the relationship the "honeymoon phase", because this is when the couple tries to win the other person over and it can be immensely exciting. They usually cannot get enough of each other – they are constantly texting, calling, meeting each other, and showering each other with thoughtful gifts. Some would say this is the most romantic part of the relationship. When getting to know a toxic person, the honeymoon phase would be more appropriately known as the "grooming phase". It feels a lot like the honeymoon phase, wherein they love bomb you and you feel as though you are on top of the world. You will start to believe that they are the perfect match for you, as they show you everything you want to see in order to fall in love with them. The difference between the honeymoon phase and the grooming phase with an emotional abuser is, however, that the motivation is not to get to know you, but is to rope you in and make you put them on a pedestal, so that you will always believe they can do no wrong.

The grooming phase is a pathway to validation for the abuser. By showering you with constant love and affection, they will expect you to reciprocate and perceive them to be the person you dreamed of. This gives them validation and reassurance that they are the perfect partner and that you will always give them the benefit of the doubt, even when they are abusing you.

If you are someone who has not learned how to love themselves, and you have codependent tendencies, then you will probably fall head over heels in love with them fairly quickly and believe that their "grooming phase" personality is their true character.

In all fairness, it is easy to fall in love and see the good in an emotional abuser, because that is all they showcase in the grooming phase. They are so charming and affectionate that you almost have no reason to doubt that they are anything but perfect – and that is their goal.

As the relationship goes on and you start to fall deeper and deeper in love with your partner, they begin to show their true colours. The toxicity, the narcissism, the manipulation, the insults, the gaslighting, and so on. All of it emerges and this leaves you dumbfounded. This is not who you were dating initially.

The person you were dating was full of love, generosity and charm. You see this other confusing side to your partner more often, and you start to question which version of your partner is real – the grooming phase version, or the current one?

If you do not truly love yourself and put yourself first, you will believe that the grooming phase version of your partner is the real one, even when his abusive behaviour is hurting you, out of fear of losing them. If you do call your partner out on their behaviour, they will feel threatened that you are standing up for yourself and that you are setting boundaries.

They will get angry that all the work they did during the grooming phase is not paying off, because you are able to see through their mask. As a result, they will manipulate and gaslight you in order to convince you that you are overreacting, and that they are doing nothing wrong.

Remember, the abuser will rarely accept blame for their actions, since they think their behaviour is valid. They will do such a good job of convincing you of this that you will start to believe them and actually justify their behaviour too. You will take what they are saying personally and apply all of that to your character, until you are completely convinced that you are the one who is overreacting and wrong, not them.

At this point, you would have excused their behaviour and they would be giving you affection again so that you do not see the need to leave them – this is how they keep you strung along; this is how the cycle begins again.

Codependency breeds a repetitive cycle of cognitive dissonance throughout the relationship. Loving yourself and setting boundaries allows you to realize that the abusive version of your partner is the real one, because you would not tolerate that kind of behaviour if you truly loved yourself.

Your boundaries would be strongly enforced and if they crossed those boundaries, you would do everything in your power to pull yourself out of the cycle and never fall into it again. Of course, it is easier said than done, but the more you consciously make the effort to put yourself first and enforce your boundaries, the more automatic this behaviour will become. Otherwise, by not loving yourself and looking for your partner to give you that love, you will lean toward believing the lovey-dovey version of your partner through positive projection – because you really want the relationship to work out and maybe have a fear of ending up alone or starting over. It will be a constant internal struggle and it will take its toll on you, almost every single time.

So, how do we get rid of cognitive dissonance?

1. Strongly enforce your boundaries

When your partner acts emotionally abusive with you, do not sweep it under the rug. You are an amazing person and you deserve better than to be treated that way. It is natural to want to see the good in your partner and let it go, but the more you do this, the more you are teaching your partner how to treat you.

You are showing them that you will tolerate any sort of behaviour and will stick by them no matter what. They will assume they can do whatever they want and you will always forgive them.

They will have the upper hand. Instead, let the love you have for yourself protect you from their abuse and stand up for yourself. If you observed someone close to you being abused, you would probably tell them they cannot allow their partner to treat them that way, your protective instincts may kick in. If you could do that for someone else, why not do that for yourself? You are the most important person in your life. Let your partner know that you are not going to tolerate their abuse and that you have boundaries they need to respect.

Learning to identify how your partner emotionally abuses you is the key to ensuring that you do not let yourself fall for their manipulation again. This way, you will see their true colours and believe them. Your cognitive dissonance will start to disappear and you will have a clear answer on what to believe.

2. Observe whether their actions and words match up

It is easy for an emotional abuser to win you over using just their words. They know you need them; they know you will not leave them. They know exactly what you want to hear in order for you to stay, so they will say just that. Emotionally abusive partners are quickly able to gauge what your insecurities are and can use these insecurities against you to make you believe that they are the only one that is going to "love" you. They will probably tell you that they will change; that they will give you the whole world and make promises they will not keep. In the moment, they seem pretty convincing and so you believe them. However, as the days go by, you notice that their actions do not match up with their words, and that is where the cognitive dissonance kicks in. You will wonder why their actions and words are so contradictory, but you will probably give them the benefit of the doubt because they have conditioned you to believe every word they say, even though your instincts are telling you otherwise.

Actions speak louder than words, and if your partner's actions are contradicting their words, then allow them to show you who they really are and believe them. It will be difficult to disentangle yourself from their web of false promises, but the moment you are able to do that, you will realize how freeing it can be.

3. *Avoid positive projection*

As mentioned earlier, positive projection from your side is as bad as insecurity projection from the abuser's side. You could be hoping to have found your soulmate, you could be running against a biological clock, you could be ready to finally settle down and feel less lonely – whatever your hope is for your love life, do not allow it to cloud your judgment.

Your positive projection will blur the line between what you truly deserve and your partner's abuse, causing you to tolerate anything they do to hurt you. Hope is a powerful emotion, however do not let it prevent you from seeing who your partner truly is. If your partner has told you they are going to propose to you at some point but they are being emotionally abusive, and you find yourself prioritizing your hope to get married to them to the extent where you are justifying their abusive behaviour, then chances are you are positively projecting and giving in to the cognitive dissonance.

Identify what strong hopes and desires you have for your love life, and recognize when you are projecting these hopes during the course of the relationship. The more you practice the art of recognition, the more clarity you will gain on your cognitive dissonance.

4. *Respond rather than react*

Your partner will do and say things that will make you emotionally vulnerable. Whether it is an insult, manipulation, gaslighting, or humiliation, you are going to feel a sting. It is only natural – you are human, you have emotions and you do have feelings for this person. You would expect them to respect you and make you feel supported, but instead they make you feel undeserving. Your cognitive dissonance can make you struggle with what to believe, and this struggle brings up feelings of anxiety, anger, sadness and anguish.

It can be intimidating to talk to an emotional abuser because of their manipulative personality, so make sure that whatever you say to them is a response rather than an emotional reaction. It is easy to get lost in your emotions and quickly react when your partner says or does something to hurt you. The best thing to do instead is to take a breath and hold onto yourself for a second. Realize that your partner is coming from a place of insecurity and dominance, whereas you have the ability to come from a place of love.

Again, be compassionate with yourself and turn on that self-love gene; take what they are saying with a pinch of salt and craft a response that will show them that you will not tolerate disrespect and that they can reach out to you when they decide to accept that. A well-thought-out response is much more effective in controlling the intensity of an argument than an emotional reaction. Remember, no matter what your partner says, take a second to think about what would be the best response and then calmly convey it to them. The skill of taking a step back will help perfect your sense of clarity during cognitive dissonance as well.

5. *Trust your gut*

If you have a gut feeling that something does not seem right, then chances are you are right. If you can sense that your partner is putting up a front and being inconsistent with the way they behave with you, then you owe it to yourself to indulge in that thought. Protecting your mental sanity is more important than anything else and sometimes it helps to clear your cognitive dissonance by trusting your instincts. You can rationalize all you want, but if you have a nagging feeling in the pit of your stomach telling you that something is wrong, then you should listen to it. Not knowing what to believe in an abusive relationship is one of the biggest factors that contribute to mental health issues, because of the constant deliberation between two opposing realities.

You do not need to settle for someone who emotionally abuses you because you do not want to be alone, or because you think you are behind on your "life's timeline". You deserve someone who does not ever let you question who they truly are and where you stand with them.

Toxic partners portray inconsistent behaviour, which breeds the beast of cognitive dissonance. It is important to find clarity during those moments and the goal is to accept the reality of what your partner is showing you at this particular moment. If they have made promises to you and have love bombed you in the past, but currently are acting intolerable, that is the version of them you need to accept. It is easy for someone to fake affection, but it is hard for them to fake abuse. If you perceive them to be abusive, they are being abusive. You have strength within you to gain the clarity you need to get rid of cognitive dissonance and the more you practice it, the easier it will get.

Write down some times when your partner's behaviour was contradictory to how they have behaved in the past.

_____

_____

_____

_____

_____

_____

_____

Recount some times when your partner's words and actions did not match up.

_____

_____

_____

_____

_____

_____

_____

In what specific situations do you find yourself struggling to figure out which version of your partner to believe?

_____

_____

_____

_____

_____

Chapter 9
Gaslighting

B eing in an emotionally abusive relationship can take a heavy toll on you. As you are learning about all the abusive tactics your partner can use on you, there is one tactic that is particularly appalling: gaslighting. If you are not too sure what gaslighting is but think you may be in an emotionally abusive relationship, this will definitely sound familiar to you. Gaslighting is when someone makes you question the validity of your own reality. They lead you to doubt things you thought you knew for certain, such as your memories, emotions, thoughts and even experiences. Self-doubt becomes second nature to you and you start to live a life of constantly questioning your perception of reality.

Once they have made you doubt what you thought you knew, they tell their side of the story. They discredit your perception of reality and enforce their version of what is true. What is unbelievable is that they are usually so convincing, that you actually start to believe their story. They do not gaslight you over huge details that are obviously unmistakable, but they do persuade you of minor details that can be easily changeable.

For example, if you were sure that you ate dinner on a red plate, your partner could easily convince you that you are wrong and that you actually ate dinner on a blue plate. They formulate such convincing arguments in their favour, that you have no choice but to believe them.

Warning signs of gaslighting:

1. Words and actions do not match

Your partner will say one thing, but do something completely on the contrary. They could say they care about you more than anything else in the world, but then treat you as though you do not hold any value to them. Or they could love bomb you for a couple of days, and then say hurtful insights to emotionally wear you down. This misalignment of words and actions causes you to constantly question what to believe and it can make you want to perceive the loving actions or words as the truth in order to soften the blow of the contradictory treatment.

2. Denial

One of the biggest signs of gaslighting is when your partner completely denies saying or doing something. They usually do this in order to prove a point, win an argument or sometimes to make themselves look innocent. They are usually so adamant in their denial that you start to question your truth and doubt whether you are remembering things correctly. This is exactly what they want you to do. It causes you confusion and as they keep denying things, your mind gets accustomed to believing their truth over yours.

3. Unmistakable lying

Lying, which goes hand-in-hand with denial, entails your partner blatantly lying to you and not backing down. You may even know the truth behind these lies, but your partner will do everything they can to convince you that they are telling the truth. Lying is a way for them to get what they want and even when you know that they are telling a huge lie, they will stand by it without any guilt.

4. Insults

In order to get you to believe them and get what they want, they will attack aspects of your character and life so that you lose your sense of identity. They say hurtful things as a retaliation to not getting what they want, and tear you down to a point where you have a low sense of self-worth. You may even start believing what they say about you, because they have ripped you of your identity and you may rely on what they tell you about yourself. The most dangerous part about this is that you start to not feel like yourself anymore, and do not know how to find yourself again.

5. *Projection*

As you have learned in Chapter 7, projection is when your partner projects their emotional wounds, insecurities and ill-treatment onto you. If they are treating you badly, they will accuse you of being the one who is treating them badly. If they are neglecting you and not giving you enough affection, they will accuse you of not giving them affection. Abusers cannot take responsibility for their actions and so use projection as a way to absolve themselves of any guilt or shame. Even if you try to remind them of something, they will take it as manipulation and accuse you of being a manipulator. They will try to paint you as themselves as much as they can.

6. *Positive reinforcement*

Positive reinforcement is a psychological concept wherein you are rewarded for taking an action. Due to the reward factor, you keep doing that action in order to keep receiving that reward. In the case of an emotionally abusive relationship, your partner will reward you for things you do that fit their agenda. If you do something that is in the best interest of the abuser, they may show you love, say nice things to you, take you out on a date, make your favourite meal, etc. They know that if they reward you when you do whatever they want, you will continue to do so in hopes for that reward.

Unfortunately, the same does not apply for when you are focusing on yourself. They will not positively reinforce anything you do for yourself, as it may not line up with what they want. Positive reinforcement is a selfish tactic they use to train you to WANT to do whatever they want. This way, they have control over you.

7. *Isolate you from your friends and family*

You will most probably not be the only victim of your partner's gaslighting. Your friends and family will also face their gaslighting in attempts to isolate you from them. The abuser will convince your social network of things that are not true – they will lie to them, and manipulate them to convince you to do what they want. They will do everything they can to get inside of their heads to make them believe that you are the problem, not them. As a result, in addition to the abuser convincing you to isolate yourself from other people, your friends and family may be convinced to leave you alone as well. This way, your partner has complete control over you, knowing that no one else can influence you to steer away from them.

When it comes to a conflict, emotional abusers use gaslighting as a way to invalidate your feelings and "win" the argument. Let's say that your partner has made a back-handed comment to insult you and that has upset you. When you try to express that emotion to them, they will use gaslighting to convince you that you are overreacting, you are the one who is insulting them, and that you have no reason to feel this way. The aim is to make you mistrust your judgment at all times so that you have to rely on them for the truth.

By relying on your partner to constantly tell you what the truth is, you lose your sense of self. You start to forget that you have your own autonomy and even if you try to rely on yourself, chances are you do not feel confident enough to believe your truth. Gaslighting is one of the most dangerous abusive tactics an abuser can use, because they are essentially snatching away your individualism. They pick away at the substance of your character until you are left with just your shell. You are the best judge of who you are, but gaslighting creates room for the abuser to step in and tell you who you are, contrary to what you believe. They eventually become the puppet master of your life.

Since gaslighting robs you of your sense of self, this abusive tactic can cause severe mental health issues, such as anxiety, depression, isolation and low self-esteem. Your mind and body can go through so much pain and it can almost feel irreversible. In order to protect yourself from gaslighting, it is important to follow these few steps:

1. *Make sure you know who you are involved with*

When you are dating someone new, it is normal to take your time and get to know them at a steady pace. You will not get to see their true colours in the first few dates, so it is important to be on the lookout for any red flags early on. This does not mean that you have to have your guard up every minute you spend with this person, but be observant of the things they say and do as you get to know them. While developing feelings for the person, be cognizant of who they are and their character traits. If you spot a trait that sits on the verge of being abusive, at least you spotted this early on and you can gauge whether this person is the right one for you.

For instance, if the person you are involved with is charming but has a tendency to consistently "correct you" when you are wrong and make you believe their version of the story, then you could hypothesize that they are gaslighting you and you will be able to identify these instances easily in the future. Even if you are already in a long-term relationship with someone, you can always start being aware now. Make a conscious effort to take note when your partner gaslights you. Identifying it is the first step.

2. *Validate your own thoughts and feelings*

The basis of gaslighting is to invalidate your truth. If you are feeling a certain way or you know something to be true, your partner will invoke self-doubt. An emotional abuser always portrays themselves to be the victim in any situation, even if they are the one who instigated it in the first place. You will probably react to their gaslighting and defend your truth, but they will turn that around to blame you for something that they did and will play the victim to absolve themselves of any responsibility for their actions. At this point, it is just your word against theirs, and unfortunately theirs always wins.

The reason they get to play the victim card and gaslight you is because you, like most people in the world, seek validation from your partner. It is normal to seek validation from other people, but there are different levels to this. Emotional abusers usually target people who need high levels of validation for almost every aspect of their life because they know these people will listen to whatever they say. Therefore, if you are someone who seeks a lot of validation from your partner, you will fall prey to their gaslighting and believe them when they say your truth is not valid – that will be the validation you accept.

Instead, if you learn to validate yourself on a daily basis, you will not need anybody else to tell you your feelings are true. No matter what your partner says, you will be able to reassure and support yourself when they are gaslighting you, which will ultimately result in you not being convinced by them. Whatever you think, feel, say or do, try telling yourself every day that your autonomy is justifiable and no one can persuade you otherwise. Even at times when your partner is being overly difficult, at least you will have your own reassurance and validation to keep you strong. You will not let go of your truth because you are all the validation you need.

3. *Make peace with the fact that they will believe whatever they want*

Toxic people rarely accept other people are right. It is either their way or the highway and this applies to gaslighting as well. No matter how much you defend yourselves to them, your partner will continue to disprove your truth. It is exhausting having to constantly prove yourself to someone who is not willing to listen, thus it is better to accept that your partner will not process whatever you try to say. They will think and say whatever they want to and there is nothing you can do about it. All you can do is take a step back and tell yourself that you know the truth. You know exactly what has happened, what was done and said, and what you are feeling. If your partner cannot accept that, that is on them and you do not need to be dragged down by their gaslighting. Chances are you are not making things up in your head and what you perceive to be reality is in fact true, so be confident with yourself and stick to that. The only person who can convince themselves of anything is you and only you.

Steps towards healing

If you have been a victim of gaslighting, you may or may not have realized how big of an effect it has had on your mental health and sanity. Being consistently told that nothing in your mind is true can really push you to question whether you are sane or not. Remember that you are sane – no matter what your partner says. Recognize that this is just an abusive tactic they are using and not the actual truth.

Healing from gaslighting will take time, as you are probably used to relying on your partner to tell you what is what, but take the time to invest in yourself. You may struggle with issues to do with shame, anger, guilt, anxiety, depression, loneliness and confusion, and this is where your first priority should be to unlearn what your partner has conditioned you to believe and start teaching yourself how to stay true to yourself.

Write down some instances when your partner made you question whether you remembered something correctly.

_____

_____

_____

_____

_____

_____

_____

_____

_____

_____

Write down some times when your partner invalidated your feelings and blamed you for the fight.

_____

_____

_____

_____

_____

_____

_____

_____

_____

_____

_____

Recount some times when your partner called you a liar when you knew you were telling the truth.

_____

_____

_____

_____

_____

_____

_____

_____

_____

_____

Have there been times when your partner made you feel "crazy" or "stupid"? Write them down.

_____

_____

_____

_____

_____

_____

_____

_____

_____

_____

_____

_____

Chapter 10:
The Silent Treatment

A t some point in your life, you probably have given or been given the silent treatment. If you are not familiar with what this is, the silent treatment is when someone deliberately does not communicate with you in order to show disapproval. It is a passive-aggressive tactic used for a prolonged period of time to show the other person that whatever they said or did was not appreciated, and that there is no more room for discussion on the matter. Most emotionally mature adults do not use the silent treatment, as this does not help solve issues effectively. They usually communicate their feelings in a healthy manner and leave things open for discussion so that they can resolve the issue. However, emotional abusers and narcissists use the silent treatment pretty often, as they know how much this affects their victim.

As you have learned, emotionally abusive partners will use multiple tactics to control you and make sure you stick around, usually during a conversation or after an argument. The silent treatment is a particularly uncomfortable strategy because the abuser knows how much it will bother you if they cut communication with you. If you are codependent on them, then your partner knows that the silent treatment will eat you up inside – the alarm bells in your mind will go off and you will beg them to talk to you again. The silent treatment can cause a lot of anxiety and should not be the go-to method of dealing with conflict. So, why do emotional abusers do it?

They do not know how to process their emotions

Chances are during a conversation or a moment with them, you may have added salt to an open emotional wound. They may or may not be aware of this internal wound, but you might have struck a chord that negatively affected them. Since toxic people are not the best at sitting with their emotions and processing how they feel, due to their tendency to avoid uncomfortable feelings, they shut down. Your partner feels hurt or angry or threatened and does not know how to deal with these feelings, so their automatic coping mechanism is to avoid interacting with you.

Poor communication skills

Communication is the key to all healthy relationships. If you are unable to communicate what you are feeling and thinking with your partner, there is room for misunderstandings and increased conflict. Since most people who are emotionally abusive did not have healthy relationships to look up to in their childhood, they also do not know how to communicate what they feel with their partner if something is bothering them. Since they do not know how to process their emotions, if you have hit one of their insecurities, then they just react without actually thinking about why they are feeling a certain way.

Furthermore, they will probably project what they are feeling onto you before they start the silent treatment, because then they have an excuse to play the victim. Your partner does not know how to take responsibility for their emotions, so they will blame you for causing the argument and make everything sound like you planned to cause them pain. This way, they have an excuse to not talk to you and make you feel guilty to the extent where you are begging for their attention and profusely apologizing. Although the environment they grew up in was not in their control and they never learned how to properly reflect on their emotions, it still does not justify them using the silent treatment with you.

They know it affects you

As hurtful as this sounds, your partner also gives you the silent treatment because they know how much it hurts you. If they know you are someone who needs their validation and attention, they will use the silent treatment as a way of getting you to sink below what your standards are in order to win back their affection. If you are self-loving and know your boundaries, you will not let yourself get dragged into the emotional entanglement they want to pull you into. You will know that this is just an abusive tactic they are using to gain some more power over you. If you show them that the silent treatment does not bother you, they will see that they cannot control you using that tactic and will end up breaking the silence sooner than expected.

They use it as a form of punishment

The silent treatment is one of the most ruthless punishments someone can use on you, because it is a breeding ground for anxiety. You may not know what you have done or said, you will not know for how long you will be frozen out, and you will start to feel abandoned. What you may not realize is that your partner is punishing you for you holding them responsible for their feelings. If you did or said something that hit a nerve, an emotionally healthy person would be able to accept that these are the feelings they are having and communicate that to you. However, an emotionally abusive person never wants to take responsibility for their emotions, so they sweep them under the rug and instead punish you for trying to get them to open their eyes about their feelings. They do not want to be held accountable for whatever they did or said during the conversation too.

How do you deal with the silent treatment?

Unfortunately, your partner will not change this tactic even if you plead them to multiple times. This is a coping strategy that has been ingrained in them for a long time and emotional abusers do not believe they need to work on themselves or change anything. So, if the silent treatment is here to stay, how should you deal with it?

1. Do not take it personally

This is easier said than done, but do not take it personally. If you are not fully secure within yourself, you will start to think that maybe your partner has abandoned you, or believe they do not think it is worth having a conversation with you, and all of these thoughts will pull you into an anxious spiral. Instead, accept that your partner is using the silent treatment because THEY do not know how to process their emotions and communicate effectively. Accept that this is an abusive tactic they are using and it has nothing to do with your self-worth.

Remove yourself from the equation, keep your head high and remember who you are, no matter how silent their treatment is. This is just them being immature and you do not need to let it bring you down. They will break their silent treatment once they see that it is not affecting you. Like a child, it is a form of gaining your attention, but if you do not give them that satisfaction, they will realize that this tactic does not work on you.

2. *Prioritize processing your own emotions*

Even though your partner does not know how to process their emotions, that does not mean that you should not make your emotions a priority. Being shut out by your partner can really sting – it is painful to experience your partner ignoring you, knowing that it is devastating you. It can make you feel unheard and invisible, and that is not how you want your partner to make you feel. Your feelings are valid and so take the time to process your emotions and thoughts. Try to identify why you feel a certain emotion or get a certain thought when a specific trigger presents itself. Being self-aware can help you grow tremendously and ultimately give you the strength to distance yourself from your partner's emotional projections. Sit with your feelings and then figure out what would be the best way to alleviate the stress you are feeling from all of this. Would a hobby help? Some meditation? Writing in a journal? Speaking to a friend? Think about what would help turn your day around, even if it is something small that you could do. Remember that you matter and your mental sanity comes first.

3. Be sure to tell your partner how you feel later

Even though you will process your emotions and accept that this is your partner's coping mechanism, it is essential that you talk about how the silent treatment made you feel when they do eventually start communicating with you again. Do not be afraid to let them know that there may be unfinished business you two need to take care of and having a conversation will be the way to do that. Also, reiterate how being shut out made you feel, as that is not your idea of a healthy communication tactic. Convey to them what emotions you felt when they shut you out and tell them how you would prefer to deal with conflict in the future. Hopefully your partner understands where you are coming from, but if they do not, even expressing your feelings out loud can be therapeutic and freeing for you.

4. Set your boundaries

This is a recurring theme, but setting boundaries is extremely important in an emotionally abusive relationship. If you do not let your partner know what you are willing to tolerate and what you have zero tolerance for, your partner will assume they can do whatever they want to hurt you with no consequences. You are in control of what you are willing to tolerate and the stronger you enforce your boundaries, the more obvious it will be to your partner that they cannot shake you. Ensure they know that it is okay to be overwhelmed at times, but after they have taken the time to cool down, they need to come back to the conversation and make sure they finish it, so that nothing seems unsettled. Again, communication is important to solving issues in a relationship, so let your partner know that this is something you need from them and that it is non-negotiable.

If you and your partner get into a heated argument, it is fine to take some space to cool off. In fact, sometimes it is necessary to in order to have a healthy and mature conversation. However, when this turns into the silent treatment, that is when trouble begins and it is crucial to take the steps needed to deal with it effectively.

Write down some instances when your partner used the silent treatment on you.

_____

_____

_____

_____

_____

_____

_____

_____

_____

_____

_____

_____

_____

_____

_____

_____

_____

_____

_____

_____

_____

_____

_____

_____

_____

_____

_____

_____

Why do you think your partner gives you the silent treatment?

_____

_____

_____

_____

_____

_____

_____

_____

_____

_____

_____

How do they eventually start communicating with you again? Is there something you need to do for this to happen?

_____

_____

_____

_____

_____

_____

_____

_____

_____

_____

_____

Part 3
Healing from Abuse

T his is the section you have been waiting for. You are possibly so tired of all the heartache and anxiety you have experienced and do not know how to be happy anymore. You have probably gone through so much pain in your current or past relationships, that you are ready to find that inner peace. This section will be your guide to healing.

From soothing the wounds to your mental health and creating a safe bubble for yourself, all the way to giving you strength and guidance should you choose to leave the relationship, this section walks you through everything step-by-step. You will learn how to recognize the amazing traits that you embody and how to love each and every aspect of yourself, even your imperfections. You will learn how to parent and support yourself throughout not only this phase of your life, but every other tumultuous phase of your life too.

Self-love is the most important kind of love, and you will come across this theme countless times throughout this section. Without self-love, your journey to healing could be stagnant. Part 3 will show you that while you are on your path to recovery, there will be difficulties on the way. Healing is not a linear journey, there will most certainly be times when you want to give up and go back to your comfort zone, but that is completely normal. This section will help you recognize your relapses and help you jump over those emotional hurdles to transport you to a stronger and more content state of mind.

You have made it this far. Keep going, you've got this.

Chapter 11
Healing from PTSD and CPTSD

Y ou may have heard about Post Traumatic Stress Disorder (PTSD) and might have also used it colloquially in a sentence to describe your state of mind after experiencing a distressing event. However, what exactly is PTSD and when does it become a serious mental illness?

PTSD is defined as a mental health condition that brings severe stress to a person following a significantly traumatic experience in their life, which include (but are not limited to) events such as being the victim of terrorism, rape, assault and war battles. When a person is removed from that traumatic situation, they experience high bouts of stress as though they are still living in that situation. Another form of PTSD is Complex Post Traumatic Stress Disorder (CPTSD). It is similar to PTSD in that it has the same symptoms plus some additional ones, however the biggest difference is that someone develops CPTSD when they have been exposed to trauma for a prolonged period of time without being able to remove themselves from the situation, whereas PTSD occurs after a shorter traumatic event. Events that can trigger CPTSD include (but are not limited to) abusive relationships, human trafficking, living in war regions, and so on. CPTSD is starting to become more recognized amongst mental health professionals, and is becoming more prevalent in victims of emotional abuse.

What are the common symptoms of PTSD and CPTSD?

The premise of both PTSD and CPTSD is reliving the traumatic event. This can manifest in multiple ways and it can show up in each person differently. Since PTSD and CPTSD are similar, here are some of the common symptoms to look out for in both:

Flashbacks and nightmares

Since these disorders thrive on making you relive the traumatic event, you may have spontaneous flashbacks of certain parts of the trauma, or it may creep into your dreams while you are sleeping and present itself as an inescapable nightmare. It will feel so real that you will probably believe that you are actually back in the traumatic environment, and your body will start to react in a manner that prepares you for the threat. If you have just gotten out of an emotionally abusive relationship, you may have dreams about the abuser or you may have random flashbacks of how they used to manipulate you and hurt you.

Avoidance

Due to the intensity of the trauma, it is natural for your mind and body to want to avoid similar situations and people. For example, if someone was the victim of a hostage situation at a supermarket, it would probably be a while before they decide to step into a grocery store again. Even if you were not a direct victim of a traumatic event, if you were watching it on the news over and over again and you empathized with the victims, it can invoke fear in you and you will need some space away from certain triggering situations. The most common side effect from getting out of an emotionally abusive relationship is avoiding relationships altogether. After going through so much pain, you will think that not getting into a relationship with anybody else will save you from that pain again and you will be safer from it.

Hyperarousal

Depending on the type of traumatic event, you may have an overly sensitive response to certain triggers. If someone is a war veteran, they may be jumpy when they hear loud noises, or if you have been in an emotionally abusive relationship before, you may have an emotional or angry outburst when you perceive someone to be manipulating you. Being easily startled, poor emotion regulation and feeling jittery are all hyper-anxiety symptoms that can manifest when your mind perceives your current situation to be similar to your trauma (even if the reality proves that it is not).

Negative thoughts and change in beliefs

After going through something traumatic in your life, chances are your perception of life will change. It is difficult to feel like yourself when a traumatic experience has left you with an abundance of painful memories and challenging emotions. It is difficult to be yourself when you have experienced trauma – the mind needs time to process it and heal. In that process, your thoughts and beliefs start to change. You may start believing that bad things happen to good people, or that nothing will ever be better again. You may even start to expect more traumatic experiences to happen to you because your mind has been conditioned to prepare yourself for further danger. What you once believed to be true in the world, may look like a distant speck in your reality. You might have had some faith or beliefs about the world that you lived by, but the nature of your trauma may have caused you to question its validity. Being a victim of emotional abuse can leave you thinking that every relationship might turn out to be as painful and that there is no hope for you to have a happy love life. These thoughts and beliefs may seem like the truth, but it is essential to remember that they can be revisited and reframed to more realistic thoughts.

Trouble sleeping and concentrating

This is when the traumatic experience consumes your life. You are constantly being reminded of it, thinking about it and fearing it may happen again. As a result, your peace of mind gets disrupted and it impairs your ability to function in daily life. The stress from the trauma keeps you up at night and prevents you from focusing on the present. The discomfort and fear that comes from being in an emotionally abusive relationship takes its toll on you, as you might be replaying the relationship in your head to analyze what else might have contributed to its demise, or living in fear that you might run into your abuser somewhere down the line. These thoughts and fears engulf you and it becomes difficult for you to live a fulfilling life.

Assigning guilt and blame to yourself

Depending on the traumatic event, you might find yourself feeling extremely guilty for the events that transpired, or you might blame yourself for certain things that happened. You may relive the experience in your mind and think that you could have done something better, or that you could have controlled the situation. In an emotionally abusive relationship, the abuser most likely projected his insecurities and wounds onto you, and blamed you for the demise of the relationship. Therefore, you would be left feeling as though the damage of the relationship falls onto your shoulders and that you did not do enough to fix the relationship or help yourself. More often than not, the trauma you experienced from the relationship was all from your abuser and you did not realize the effects of them until after, so it is important to not be so hard on yourself.

Dissociation

Sometimes, our minds are unable to cope with trauma. The traumatic event could be so devastating, that our minds decide to turn a blind eye to its effects. The way it does this is by disconnecting your awareness of the trauma in order to protect your conscious. For example, a child being physically abused by their father would probably use dissociation as a coping mechanism to escape from the reality of their situation. It can feel as though your mind is separated from your body or you may feel numb to certain things because your mind is not processing what is happening. You are simply watching your life happen without actually being present in it. You may experience dissociation if the abuse in your relationship was far too extreme and intense. Episodes of physical and sexual abuse can cause dissociation and it can be arduous to heal from it. This may not manifest as easily in everybody, but it is a symptom that could occur in some.

Physical symptoms

Most of the time, PTSD and CPTSD sufferers sweep their traumatic experiences under the rug so that they do not have to confront them. By doing so, they are certainly safe from the stress it brings in that specific moment, but the subconscious has an interesting way of bringing suppressed trauma to the forefront in some manner. If your conscious mind does not allow your subconscious to bring up those memories, the stress from your trauma can manifest in physical symptoms. These psychosomatic symptoms may include dizziness, headaches, nausea, pain, rapid heart rate, shallow breathing and sweating. When the mind holds on to traumatic experiences, our body tends to project these experiences in different ways. If you have chosen to suppress the abuse you experienced in your toxic relationship, then chances are those will come out at some point in the form of any of these physical symptoms. Prolonged stress is never suitable for the body and if you do not face it head on, you could be lengthening the healing process. If you are able to process your trauma and heal from it, the physical symptoms tend to disappear as well.

Additional symptoms of CPTSD

CPTSD has a few additional symptoms that emerge due to the prolonged time of trauma. These symptoms include:

Low self-esteem and self-worth

Experiencing trauma for a long time, especially in an abusive relationship, can increase your tolerance for stress. However, it also takes a toll on your confidence and can lower your sense of self-worth and your self-esteem. An emotionally abusive relationship will have you questioning whether you are good enough to be loved, or whether you can handle difficult things in life. Once the relationship is over, you will probably still carry this low sense of self-worth into other aspects of your life because your partner convinced you of these false notions throughout the relationship.

Trouble maintaining relationships

CPTSD brings with it a tremendous amount of stress that can be overwhelming. As a result, you might not have the motivation or the mental strength to keep up with certain parts of your life, especially with your relationships. It can be tiresome to put on a smile and interact with other people when you have so much emotional pain to deal with, and that is okay. You are allowed to feel what you feel – you went through trauma. The key here is to recognize when this starts affecting your relationships with the most important people in your life and get some support to help you through it. If you have been emotionally abused in the past, new relationships might not be easy for you to form or to maintain due to triggers of the past, however once you work on healing your emotional wounds, it can become easier for you to nurture your new relationships.

Obsessive thoughts

Since the trauma lasted for a long period of time, your brain perceives it to be a regular part of your life. Once that trauma is removed, your brain might still look for that trauma because of its familiarity. Due to this, you might indulge in obsessive thoughts and behaviours with regards to the traumatic event. For example, if your partner used to gaslight you and manipulate you, then you might indulge in obsessive thoughts about what they did wrong in the relationship, or how to exact revenge on them, or how you can avoid seeing them ever again in the future. You might do a lot of research in this area or you might stalk their social media profile to ensure that they are nowhere close to where you are now. Your mind might be so used to the trauma they put you through for so long, that it might look for it in some form or another through your thoughts. Shifting your attention to other aspects of your life is important here, so that these thoughts and behaviours do not consume your life and keep you in a traumatic state.

Do you experience any symptoms of PTSD/CPTSD? Write them down.

_____

_____

_____

_____

_____

_____

_____

_____

_____

_____

_____

What are the specific triggers that activate your symptoms?

_____

_____

_____

_____

_____

_____

_____

_____

_____

_____

_____

_____

_____

Trauma and the brain

PTSD and CPTSD consume so much of your life; it is normal to wonder where the trauma gets stored and how these mental health conditions come about. A traumatic experience is usually stored in the amygdala, which is part of the limbic system. The amygdala is the center for emotion processing and emotional regulation. If you have experienced trauma, the amygdala will remember this experience due to its highly emotional component and hide it deep within itself. The amygdala then perceives this traumatic experience as a threat to your life, and sends a signal to the adrenal glands. The adrenal glands release adrenaline in order to prepare you for danger. Adrenaline is the hormone that prepares you for "fight or flight", which means that it either prepares you to fight the danger head on, or run away from it to protect yourself. This activation of the fight or flight response triggers a response and this is when you start to feel panic or anxiety.

Anxiety is needed so that you can quickly identify a potential threat to your life – but is the threat real or not? That is what your mind has to analyze and decide. Your fight or flight response will be activated if you saw a lion inching its way toward you and roaring – that is an actual threat to your life. However, if you were sitting at home reading a book before bed and your mind decided to toss up the memory of your abuser insulting you in front of all your friends, that would definitely cause anxiety, but it would not be an immediate threat to your life. PTSD and CPTSD are known to perceive more situations in life as real threats, even when they are not, in order to protect you from similar trauma, which results in you being more hypervigilant and stressed about your present reality.

If you are not aware of your PTSD or CPTSD, your trauma could manifest itself in your dreams. You might dream of your abusive partner, or dream that you are in another abusive relationship that is presenting all the same trauma to you again. It can get to a point where you are afraid to fall asleep because you do not want to go through this additional trauma while you are sleeping. What is terrifying about having traumatic dreams is that you are unable to wake yourself up most of the time (unless you are a master of lucid dreaming) and you will be experiencing the entirety of that trauma in the nightmare. Once you wake up, you may ruminate on the nightmare and think about it during the day. Ultimately, you are under stress 24/7, which is the most exhausting life to live.

The reason you feel all these symptoms is because your brain is linking your past trauma to your present situation. Think of it as though your brain is an electric fuse box, and is short-circuiting over the smallest trigger. It needs to be rewired to learn that it does not need to short-circuit when these triggers pop up. Your mind needs to be reassured and trained to not link your past to your present.

So, how do we heal from PTSD or CPTSD and unlink your present reality from the trauma?

1. Desensitization

One way to heal your post-trauma symptoms is to desensitize yourself to the triggers. For example, if you start to panic and feel anxious when you see a photo of the abuser, desensitizing your anxious response to that trigger would help you remove yourself from that state of mind. The best way to do this is to expose yourself to certain triggers, and then breathe through them. You could look at a photo of the abuser and when you start to feel your heart rate pick up, your breathing become shallow or your palms become sweaty, you can try taking a deep breath in for 5 seconds, and then exhaling for another 5 seconds. Repeating this deep breathing exercise while looking at the photo will signal to your brain that you are not in immediate danger and that this trigger does not warrant a fight or flight response. If some other trigger pops up, in addition to deep breathing, you can engage in some loving self-talk to reassure yourself that you are okay, you are safe, and that you are a strong person.

2. Seek professional help and medication (if needed)

PTSD and CPTSD can be monstrous disorders and it can feel almost impossible to conquer on your own. Obtaining professional help from a therapist is a great step toward recovery, as they can guide you throughout the journey and you will not feel like you need to do this alone. If your psychiatrist believes medication might help you, they could prescribe you with supportive medication to relieve the intensity of your symptoms while you continue therapy.

3. Create space for the symptoms

If you do not have the resources or accessibility to consult a therapist, there are ways you can counsel yourself. In addition to desensitization, the first thing you need to tell yourself is to allow the symptoms to be there. We are programmed to want to fight against anything that makes us feel unsafe, but sometimes that can make things feel even worse. Simply accepting and allowing the symptoms to be there can make the stress feel lighter. Accept that there are some triggers that will make you react in a certain way, and that these reactions may be uncomfortable but they are not life-threatening. Once you have made room for the symptoms, start to ask yourself why you have reacted this way. What is the exact trigger? What are you afraid might happen? What thoughts cross your mind when you face this trigger? What can you say to reassure yourself that you are safe?

Living with PTSD or CPTSD is an uphill battle, but it is a battle you can definitely win with the right guidance and coping mechanisms. You have been through real trauma and you are out of it now, so remind yourself that you are safe and that you can get through this. Your mind is scared and on high alert so that you stay safe – once your mind believes that you are already safe, your mental health will start to get better.

If you experience symptoms, what steps can you take in your daily life to help yourself heal from PTSD/CPTSD?

Chapter 12
How to protect yourself from being manipulated

E motional abusers are mainly concerned with getting what they want, no matter what. They use multiple abusive tactics to make you cave and cater to their needs, and one such tactic is manipulation. Manipulation is especially treacherous because your partner is an expert at disguising their manipulation as sincerity, and you will not always know when they are actually manipulating you.

Your partner will continue to use manipulative tactics on you to get what they want, unfortunately there is nothing you can do to stop them from doing that. It is in their nature. However, while you learn how to recognize manipulation, it is even more important to look inside yourself and identify what is allowing you to be manipulated.

Is it codependency? Need for validation? Fear? Once you know why you allow your partner to manipulate you, you can work on healing those wounds within yourself so that you are no longer an easy target for manipulation.

Here are five manipulation tactics the emotional abuser likely uses on you and how to protect yourself from each one:

1. *Guilt, shame and blame*

Your partner will ask you for something that they want you to do for them, and if you are not comfortable, you will say no. A healthy partner would respect your response, they may not like that you said no, but they will leave it at that and be accepting of your decision. An abuser will not take this rejection well. They will start to question why you said no – if someone loves you and respects you, they will not always need an explanation as to why you are saying no, but an abuser will not be able to take no for an answer and will keep asking you to justify your rejection.

They will start to guilt you into feeling as though you do not love them – that you are intentionally not doing what they want because you do not care about them. They may shame you by saying that if the tables were turned, they would do anything and everything for you, and that you are not as giving. This is probably a false claim, but they say it so that you feel ashamed and give in to what they want. If you say no to doing something for them, they could blame you for their failures of not being able to do it themselves and guilt-trip you by saying they have no one else to do it for them. By guilt-tripping, shaming and blaming, they are essentially disrespecting you and not allowing you to enforce your boundary.

If you are not aware of when they are making you feel this way, and if you are codependent or insecure, you will probably allow them to say all of these things to you and you will accept it as the truth. When you say no and they push back with this particular tactic, your codependency on them will make you break your boundaries and eventually say yes to whatever it is they are asking for. You may also want to avoid confrontation or any sort of conflict, so you will completely disregard your boundaries and do whatever they want you to.

Even though they are going to push you to feel guilty, shameful and accept the blame, it does not mean that these feelings are a source of truth coming from within you.

Your partner is making you feel this way so that THEY get what they want, they will say whatever they need to make you feel uncomfortable and give in. To protect yourself from this tactic, it is best to remember that you are not actually the person they are portraying you to be, and that you need to hold your ground and keep saying no. Your decision is more important than what they want.

Can you recount some episodes when your partner tried to blame, shame and guilt-trip you into giving them what they want?

_____

_____

_____

_____

_____

_____

_____

_____

_____

_____

2. *Pressure you for an answer*

Growing up, emotional abusers did not learn how to take no for an answer. They usually got what they wanted through some method or another and they usually got it immediately. If your partner asks you for something and you say you need some time to think about it, this will not bode well for you. Unless the situation is urgent, it is never okay to pressure someone into giving an answer immediately. You have the right to take your time and space to reflect. It is difficult to make certain decisions quickly and it is completely fine to ask for some time.

An emotional abuser, on the other hand, will not understand why you need time, because they assume that you are supposed to give them what they want regardless of how you feel. They will not even give you time to think – they will keep pressuring you to say yes. They only think about what they want and disregard your need for space and privacy to think. If they cannot accept your answer of needing some time, then tell them the answer is no, because chances are the more you tell them you need time, the more they are going to bully you into saying yes, and you eventually will.

To safeguard yourself, say no right off the bat if they keep pressuring you. And stick to it. They will probably perceive your rejection as a form of disrespect towards their needs, however remember that they did not respect your need for time and space either. Put yourself first in these situations and do not back down just because of your need for their affection and validation.

Write down some times when your partner pressured you into saying yes to something immediately.

_____
_____
_____
_____
_____
_____
_____
_____
_____
_____
_____
_____
_____
_____
_____
_____
_____
_____
_____
_____

3. *Playing the victim card*

Another form of manipulation, and this is one of the abuser's favourites, is to play the victim card. Let's say your partner has asked you to skip a day of work to spend time with them. Unless you have unlimited paid days off, you will probably say you need to go to work but that you will spend time with them after work. Of course, they will not accept this answer because it is not giving them what they want, so they will keep pressuring you. You will probably start to feel guilty but you will keep saying it is not possible for you to skip work today. At this point, your partner may say that "you never want to spend time with them" and that you always "make them feel neglected". They start to accuse you of not loving them and they will make themselves out to be the victim.

If you do not allow them to pull you into this manipulation, you will see that you did not do anything wrong, and that you told them rationally why you cannot skip work today. However, if you are an extremely empathetic person with codependent tendencies who seeks validation and affection from your partner, then you will probably start to feel guilty and believe that you are the villain in this situation for saying no and going to work. As a result, you might actually end up staying home from work or feeling extremely horrible about yourself for leaving them. This is not healthy relationship behaviour – just because your partner did not get what they want, they painted themselves to be the victim and made you out to be the bad guy, when all you were doing was enforcing your boundaries.

If your partner plays the victim card, remind yourself that they are only doing this so that you give them what they want. They want you to let go of your independent decision-making skills and focus all your attention on them. Break free from their control and stay true to your boundaries. It may upset them further, but what you want is a priority too.

Can you remember some instances when your partner played the victim when you said no to something they wanted?

_____

_____

_____

_____

_____

_____

_____

_____

_____

_____

_____

_____

4. Negotiation

This is when your partner will sink to lying to get what they want from you. An emotional abuser has studied their target well enough to know what makes them tick – their insecurities, emotional wounds, their needs and their fears. Your partner will use this information to manipulate you into giving them what they want. If they know you seek their affection and need romance to feel validated, they could make a false promise and say they will take you out on the most romantic date if you said yes to what they are asking for. They have the ability to sound so sincere and honest, that you will probably believe them and give in to what they are asking for. Unfortunately, you will realize that once you give them what they want, they do not hold their end of the deal. The promises they made you hardly come to fruition because they will always have an excuse for not keeping their word.

Emotional abusers have a talent for showing you that they are honest and emotionally healthy, so it is understandable why you might believe them when they tell you these lies. Thus, it is hard for you to accept that they are manipulative, because that would be contrary to what they are showing you. However, the sad truth of the matter is that they do not know how to be in a mutually respectful relationship and they assume that the relationship should cater to all of their needs only.

It is crucial that you recognize when they are trying to negotiate with you to get something out of you. Once you acknowledge it, it will be easier for you to reject their proposal because you will know that you will not get anything from that deal. If you want to say no to them, say no to them. Even though you are in a relationship with an emotional abuser, what YOU want and what YOU are comfortable with is what matters first.

Has your partner negotiated with you and failed to deliver on their promises? Write down some examples.

_____
_____
_____
_____
_____
_____
_____
_____
_____
_____
_____
_____
_____
_____
_____

5. *Bullying*

This is probably the most difficult part of manipulation you will have to handle. Emotional abusers bully you when you have consistently said no to what they want. They are like little children – they have not learned emotional reasoning and so when they are told no, they throw a tantrum. They may not lie on the floor kicking and screaming, but they will do the adult equivalent of that. This may look like name-calling, threats, insults, and in some cases maybe even physical abuse. They are not able to process rejection and this is their way of acting out. It is a way of essentially forcing you to give them what they want.

Clearly, this type of behaviour is not acceptable, especially when you have said no. If they engage in bullying and are not able to respect your answer, then create a safe bubble for yourself. Pretend you are in a protective bubble and choose not to engage with your partner. That protective bubble can be in the form of keeping your distance from them for a little while, or meditation, or even simply telling yourself not to engage. The bubble is important because you do have feelings for this person, and once they start bullying you, it can cause you so much emotional pain that you may start to spiral. The bubble is essential for your own sanity and mental wellbeing. When you choose not to engage with your partner, they will eventually see that you are confident and nothing they do can pull you away from your boundaries and your values. This, of course, takes practice, so make sure you encourage yourself throughout the process. You will become stronger and you will become a master at putting your mental sanity first.

Write down some episodes when your partner bullied you because you did not give them what they want.

_____

_____

_____

_____

_____

_____

_____

_____

_____

_____

_____

Love yourself throughout this journey. Manipulation is a form of betrayal and that can really sting your heart. No one likes to be taken advantage of and everyone wants to be with someone who respects them and truly loves them. In order to pull yourself out of this abusive cycle, be vigilant of these manipulative tactics and if you observe your partner using any, then stay strong. Stick to your decision and do not allow your partner to sway you. Take this emotionally abusive relationship as a lesson – your partner will throw unbelievably difficult stimuli at you and it is up to you to navigate through them as best you can. Learn from all the pain and grow into a confident person. Work on your emotional wounds at the same time so that you do not feel the need to give in to their manipulation. Validate yourself, respect yourself and reassure yourself. The most important form of love is self-love.

What boundaries would you like to set with your partner?
How do you plan to enforce them from now on?

_____
_____
_____
_____
_____
_____
_____
_____
_____
_____
_____
_____
_____
_____
_____
_____
_____
_____
_____
_____
_____
_____
_____
_____
_____
_____
_____
_____

Chapter 13
How to distance yourself from an emotional abuser

B y now, you have a better idea of all the tactics that emotional abusers use to control you and get what they want from you. Knowing just how much damage emotional abuse can inflict can be enough for someone to want to leave the relationship, however sometimes it is not always possible. There may be situational factors that are preventing you from leaving your partner, such as children, legal issues, financial constraints, and so on. In these cases, you can feel trapped and suffocated knowing that you may not have an easy way out. The good news is there are ways you can distance yourself from the abuser and reduce the impact the relationship has on you, without having to cut them out completely.

Emotional abusers have spent their whole lives being abusive and expecting everything to go according to their whims and fancies, thus it is unrealistic to expect them to change. They especially do not have the innate ability to change because they genuinely do not think they are in the wrong. Since you are not able to influence change in them, you will have to accept that you have no control over how your partner behaves with you. They will be emotionally abusive if they want and there probably is not anything you can do about it. It is a tough pill to swallow, but is necessary to take. Your partner has their own path and emotional maturity, but so do you. They are not your responsibility to change, and once you accept that, you will feel less caged. Instead, focus your time and energy on yourself, you can change yourself for the better to set your boundaries and practice self-love. This is the change you should strive for - within you, not them, and this will help you distance yourself from them.

What are the steps to distancing yourself from an emotion-ally abusive partner?

_____

_____

_____

_____

_____

_____

_____

_____

_____

_____

1. *Raise your self-awareness*

As you learn more about what abusive people do, you will most likely start to recognize who in your life exhibits abusive behaviour. Your partner may be the closest one to you, but there may also be others in your life that you will come across. Being aware of what emotional abusers do is the most important first step to distancing yourself from them, because if you are not aware of what they are doing, then you will not be able to protect yourself.

Be aware of your own insecurities and emotional injuries too – what do you currently struggle with? What do you fear? When do you usually feel most vulnerable? What do you need to feel validated? Being aware of your emotional wounds will help you understand how and why you react to your partner's abuse. Observe what they do that pushes you over the edge and makes you react emotionally. What insecurities of yours make you react this way? Being aware of their actions and your reactions helps you figure out what your triggers are.

If you touch an open wound, it hurts, but if you touch it once it is healed, it will not be susceptible to as much pain. Once you know what your triggers are and you are aware of how you react to your abuser's behaviour, you can start to work on healing your wounds so that you do not react as emotionally when your partner does push those buttons. When those wounds are healed, their abuse will not affect you that much, and you probably will not give them the reaction they hope for.

What emotional wounds do you think you have from your relationship and from life in general?

_____

_____

_____

_____

_____

_____

_____

In what ways do your emotional wounds influence the way you react to your partner's abuse?

_____

_____

_____

_____

_____

_____

_____

_____

_____

2. Educate yourself on emotional abusers

As you are doing right now, informing yourself of emotional abuse is key to distancing yourself from toxic people. The more you know about how they operate, what tactics they use and what motivates them, the more leverage you will have to protect yourself. You will almost be able to predict what this person will do or how this person will react. Accordingly, you will also know how to deal with them. It helps to read up on emotional abuse and keep track of the behaviours that your partner engages in. This way, you will remember what tactics your partner uses to abuse you and you will know not to fall for them. You will be able to create a shield for yourself that protects you from their particular abusive tactics.

How does your partner abuse you? Write down all the tactics they use and when they usually use them.

_____

_____

_____

_____

_____

_____

_____

_____

_____

_____

_____

_____

_____

_____

_____

3. *Enforce your boundaries*

This is a repeated piece of advice in this workbook, but is one of the most important things you need to do to distance yourself from your abuser. Your partner will do whatever they can to get what they want from you, and if you break your boundaries in order to give it to them, they will perceive you to be weak and assume they can walk all over you without any consequences. Your partner is almost like a child – they will continue to act the way that they do, unless they are presented with consequences. It may not completely eradicate their behaviour since it is so innate, but it can show them that you are not someone who is going to sit back and allow them to rule your life.

Protecting your boundaries is an essential component of self-love. It ensures that you recognize what you need in order to live a healthy and fruitful life, and sometimes that means you have to say no. If you do not do this, you are disregarding your mental health by not giving yourself what you need. Self-love is all about providing yourself with validation, protection, happiness and fulfillment. However, if you continue to let your partner drain you of your self-love and take it for themselves, you will feel empty and drained out. Make yourself a priority and do not be afraid to say no. And stick to it.

What boundaries can you enforce with your partner?

_____
_____
_____
_____
_____
_____
_____
_____

4. *Minimize telling them about your life*

This may seem odd, as your partner should be the person you share everything with. However, if your partner is toxic, you are better off keeping things to yourself for the most part. A healthy relationship entails both partners openly communicating and sharing experiences with each other. Learning more about the other person and their life allows you to form a deeper bond and help them grow as well. However, emotional abusers take the information you give them and use it against you. If they know things such as your schedule, your fears, your vulnerabilities, then they can easily use these pieces of information to manipulate you and control you. They may sound convincing when they say you can trust them, but chances are they are only saying this so that you tell them what they need to know to gain more leverage over you.

The best way to deal with this is to say vague, generic statements and not reveal much detail. In fact, you can ask them questions about their life and they will happily answer. Emotional abusers have narcissistic traits and would love to fill their time by thinking and talking about themselves. By doing this, you are successfully shifting their attention away from you and onto themselves, and you are released from potential abuse.

What personal details about your life or yourself have you told your partner?

_____

_____

_____

_____

_____

_____

_____

_____

_____

_____

How have they used what you have told them against you?

_____

_____

_____

_____

_____

_____

_____

_____

_____

_____

5. Emotionally shield yourself

It is inevitable that you will feel incredibly hurt when your partner emotionally abuses you. You are human and you will feel distraught when the person you love treats you horribly. When the abuse is happening, the only person who can come to your rescue is you, nobody else. You will be depending on yourself to stand on your own two feet and protect yourself from any emotional damage your partner is trying to inflict on you. The tools you will need for your emotional shield are self-love, self-compassion, knowledge on emotional abuse and self-validation. By giving yourself love and validation, and telling yourself that you will be okay and that this is not your fault, you will have the strength to protect yourself, because you will be rooting for yourself.

When you have knowledge on emotional abuse, you will be able to quickly identify when your abuser is using their tactics on you and you will be able to set your boundaries. The more you carry your shield with you, the less time it will sting when your partner abuses you. Your shield is your source of power and holding that with you will make you realize how strong you really are. You will start to realize that all the abuse and hurt your partner is inflicting on you are all manifestations of their insecurities, their emotional immaturity and their projections. The abuse has nothing to do with you, and has all to do with them. When you keep reminding yourself of that, your shield will maintain your distance from your abuser and will protect you from getting tangled into their manipulation.

What things can you do for yourself to become emotionally strong?

_____

_____

_____

_____

_____

_____

_____

_____

_____

_____

_____

Evaluate your situation

All of these methods are useful when you are unable to leave your partner and have to keep your sanity and safety in check. However, you are the best judge of your situation, and if you think you would be better off without this person in your life, that is your call. You deserve to be happy, so you have every right to choose who you want in your life and who you think drains your energy. If you think your partner is too toxic and is making your days unbearable, then you should prioritize yourself and find a way to leave. Losing yourself in this relationship will only hurt you in the end, nobody else. It will be painful to cut this person out of your life, but doing that will ultimately bring you happiness and will make you feel whole again. Remove them from your life and surround yourself with people who support you, genuinely love you and help you see the beautiful things life has to offer.

Write down the pros and cons of staying in your current relationship and see which one has more points.

Pros:

_____

_____

_____

_____

_____

_____

_____

_____

_____

_____

Cons:

_____

_____

_____

_____

_____

_____

_____

_____

_____

_____

Chapter 14
How to enforce boundaries with a toxic person

T ime and time again, your partner has pushed you to your limits and crossed the line. You try to stand up for yourself but they always end up overpowering you, resulting in you having to concede. It is no secret that toxic people are insanely difficult to deal with – setting boundaries may be easy but enforcing them can seem impossible when you are faced with an emotional abuser. They manipulate you to believe that whatever they do is justified and that you are overreacting when you set a boundary. It can feel like an unwinnable plight, but it does not have to be this way.

Setting the boundary is easy, it is enforcing it that takes hard work. If you find yourself neglecting your boundaries, this could be due to these two reasons:

1. You have never properly set boundaries because you may be codependent on other people, you may be a people-pleaser because you do not want to lose anybody or you are not sure who you are and what you need.
2. You are dealing with someone extremely toxic who can convince you out of your boundaries as good as the devil can. They do not respect you and whatever they say goes. They push you past your limits to get what they want out of you.

Emotional abusers have a sort of "sixth sense" about who they target. They can tell if you have low standards and are not able to set boundaries for yourself. They can tell if you have insecurities that cut deep and have low self-esteem. Since they know that they can mold you into doing what they want, they target you.

Being emotionally abused is agonizing, but it forces you to learn the lessons. Every situation in your life is a lesson, and you will either be the student or the teacher. You may learn new skills from a certain situation, or teach someone else the skills they are meant to learn at that point in their life. Sadness, anger, happiness, guilt, shame, fear, love, and so on are all just side effects of those lessons. These emotions are by-products of the main aim which is to learn the lessons of life. In your emotionally abusive relationship, it is an opportunity to learn how to enforce your boundaries and become more confident.

So, how do you enforce boundaries?

1. *What are your current standards?*

Take a look in the mirror and figure out what your current standards are. If you do not deem something as disrespectful, then you will be disrespected. Ask yourself how much you are willing to tolerate. Have there been times when your partner has clearly violated your boundary but you have tolerated it? No matter how manipulative your partner is, if you do not love and respect yourself, then you will continue to allow them to cross the line. It is the bitter truth – if you take everything that is thrown at you, then you will continue to be abused. It will become second nature to you and you may come to a point where you will not know what is acceptable to tolerate and what is not.

If you do not speak up about their violations, they will take your silence as permission to keep overstepping. The most common reasons for victims to keep their standards low are because they either fear that the person will leave their life if they enforce those boundaries on them, or they do not want to be judged and want to avoid confrontation with the person as much as possible. If this sounds familiar to you, you are not alone. However, when you do identify what you deem disrespectful and how you want to be treated, you will realize that healthy people who are worth keeping in your life will adhere to these boundaries and stay.

If your partner does not respect your boundaries and they leave, you might be better off without them. The fear of being alone makes you conform to what the toxic person wants to do, without realizing that you are neglecting your own boundaries. Therefore, take a moment to self-reflect. Figure out what you tolerate and what you truly deem as disrespectful, without considering your partner's needs. Once you know that, you can move on to setting and enforcing those boundaries.

Throughout your life, have you set any boundaries for people? What were they?

_____

_____

_____

_____

_____

_____

_____

_____

_____

_____

What boundaries are you currently allowing your partner to cross?

_____

_____

_____

_____

_____

_____

_____

_____

_____

Write down some episodes when your partner violated some of your boundaries.

_____
_____
_____
_____
_____
_____
_____
_____
_____

How did it make you feel when your partner did not respect your boundaries?

_____
_____
_____
_____
_____
_____
_____
_____
_____
_____
_____
_____

2. *Communicate what your boundaries are*

It is one thing to set your boundaries in your mind, but that means nothing if you do not communicate them to your partner. In a calm, rational and loving manner, convey what you expect from someone who wants to be a significant part of your life. You want them to know that you love them and it matters to you that they are a part of your life, but in order to stay in your life, you have certain standards that they must meet for you to feel respected.

The way you communicate your standards is also important. If they push your limits and you communicate your boundaries emotionally during a fight, chances are they will just take this as an emotional outburst that will die down. Their ego is a condescending entity which will usually think your emotions are "over-the-top". However, if you communicate your boundaries from a place of love and confidence, they could possibly listen. Let them know that you are not trying to be difficult, but just that you love and respect yourself so much that you know how you deserve to be treated, and you will not tolerate anything less. The more you practice this, the easier it gets.

Healthy people will understand your boundaries and respect them, even if they do not like them. Toxic people, as you know, might not take you seriously at first. They might assume that you are just speaking empty words and that you will do anything for them to keep them in your life. However, if you stand your ground and they still cannot adhere to your boundaries, they will probably leave because they know they cannot control you. It will hurt if they do leave, but if you love yourself more, you will know that this is for the best and that you wish them well. Maybe, they are not the one for you.

How do you want to be treated in a relationship?

_____
_____
_____
_____
_____
_____
_____
_____
_____
_____
_____

If you were to communicate your boundaries to your partner in a loving way, how would you say it? Practice here.

_____
_____
_____
_____
_____
_____
_____
_____
_____
_____
_____
_____

3. *There must be consequences*

When you were in elementary school, you probably followed the rules because otherwise you would face punishment. You probably took these rules seriously because your teachers put the punishment to practice. You saw it happen, and so you believed it to be true. The same applies for your boundaries in a relationship. Now, this is not to say that your relationship resembles an elementary school classroom, but the principles are the same. If your partner ignores your boundaries, they will know you are being serious if you give them a consequence for their actions. Whatever the consequence might be, your partner will know you mean business.

Some toxic people will still continue to disrespect your boundaries, and this is when you need to decide if this person is worth having in your life. Do not conform to their pressure of how they think they should treat you; never let go of what you stand for. You are in charge of your life and you should not have to change your values and standards just because someone is not mature enough to understand where you are coming from.

Healthy relationships involve equal compromise from both sides – compromise is when both partners negotiate and meet each other in the middle. When you compromise, you are not abandoning your values and standards, you are simply making a small adjustment to meet your partner halfway. In an emotionally abusive relationship, you are usually the one compromising and bending over backwards because your partner does not take your boundaries seriously. If you do not enforce your boundaries, they start to think of you as "weak" and take advantage of you.

When you give someone so much and do not get the same amount of respect in return, you start to feel empty. Downplaying your standards and excusing the other person for their behaviour makes you start to believe that your standards hold no value. This is definitely not true. Therefore, hold your standards high and stick to them.

If your partner disrespected your boundaries, what would be the consequences?

If your partner cannot respect your boundaries and they leave, that is on them, not you. Do not ever believe that you made them leave because you were being "difficult". They left because they did not have the courage to be with someone who considers them their equal. You deserve someone amazing who respects you. Of course, it is always painful to let go of a relationship, so if that happens, remember to parent yourself throughout that process. Be there for yourself and love yourself. Loving yourself will fill that void you feel in your heart. Letting go is painful, but keeping them would have made you let go of yourself, which is even worse.

What has to happen for you to decide to let go of someone who has violated your boundaries?

Chapter 15
How do you leave an emotionally abusive relationship?

T his is the most commonly asked question by victims in emotionally abusive relationships. You may have told yourself countless times that you will leave this relationship and you might have also thought about all the ways in which you would do it, but somehow your fears of the future, your partner's reaction and your feelings for this person would have stopped that motivation from becoming a firm decision.

It almost feels like you are in quicksand – you want to get out and no matter how much you try to get out of it, it continues to pull you deeper and deeper into the mess. No matter how much you have gone over each scenario in your head, you end up staying in the relationship for some reason or another. It feels agonizing to even think about leaving the relationship because you possibly still have some feelings for them and you have invested so much of your time and energy into this relationship. You might still even hope that they can change and that you might be giving up too soon. If you have been waiting for things to change and you do not see a light at the end of the tunnel anytime soon, chances are they are not going to change. This becomes your signal to break it off with this person and move forward with your life.

So, how do you finally leave an emotionally abusive relationship?

1. *Make a firm and final decision to leave*

You have probably gone back and forth multiple times about if and how you should leave your partner, and you have found a reason to stay every time. This time, things need to be different. If you do not see your partner changing (and chances are they will not) and they are giving you more pain than happiness, you need to realize that this is a clear justification for you to leave. There is nothing beneficial that can happen to you by staying in this relationship.

Reflect on the damage this relationship has done to you – what it has made you afraid of, what it has made you insecure about, how you have changed as a person since you have been in this relationship. Introspect and see what internal struggles you had in the first place that made you want to stay in the relationship, even though it was toxic for you. Ask yourself why you were so afraid to leave and once you get that answer, you will know what you need to work on. After introspecting, you will realize that your wounds are making you stay, but if you heal your wounds, you will not feel the need to. Think about what you need in order to feel safe, secure, happy and validated. Is this person giving you what you need? If the answer is no, you will recognize that the logical thing to do would be to leave. Once you make a firm decision, stick to it. It is final and there is no going back.

It is usually the fear of uncertainty and pain that holds one back from leaving a partner. You might be worried about how you will move on from them, or if you will find anybody else who will love you. If you have children with this person, you might worry about what this would do to them and decide it is better for you to tolerate the abuse for the sake of your children. If you are financially dependent on this person, you might worry about how you will support yourself if you were to leave. All of these worries are valid, but they do not have to hold you back from making the right decision for yourself. If you think external factors make it almost impossible for you to leave, think again. There is always a solution to each problem, you just need to believe that you will be okay. No matter what.

The strength and determination to leave is within you, you have always had it, you just tend to focus on your fears of leaving rather than your strength to do it. Shift your focus to your strengths and encourage yourself. Self-soothing will be really important in this step of your journey. You will be scared of making that decision, but once you do, be compassionate with yourself and tell yourself you will be okay and that you are making the right decision, because you definitely are. Make the decision to turn your life around and put yourself first. Once you get rid of the toxicity in your life, you can make room for better opportunities to come by.

What do you need to feel loved and validated? What do you look for in a partner? Are you currently getting those things from your partner?

_____

_____

_____

_____

_____

_____

_____

_____

What emotional wounds do you have that are keeping you in this cycle?

_____

_____

_____

_____

_____

_____

_____

_____

_____

2. *Prepare yourself for your partner's reaction*

You know your partner well enough by now. When you break the news to them, you can expect them to lash out and be even more abusive towards you, because they are not going to like what you just told them. Mentally and physically prepare yourself for their reaction.

Brace yourself for an influx of their abusive tactics, as they will now see that you are standing on your own two feet and they are losing their control over you. They will do whatever they can to make you feel as low as you possibly can and will say whatever they need to in order to get you to stay. No matter what happens though, stick to your guns and remember that this person is not going to change. You have given them multiple chances and they have proven they cannot do it every single time.

Give yourself as much encouragement, confidence and love before you tell them you are leaving. You will need a lot of strength during this conversation and you need to ensure that you will not cave and fall prey to their abusive tactics. Working on yourself and healing your wounds will give you the strength to go through with this conversation. They might blame you, shame you, insult you, gaslight you and project all of their insecurities onto you. They may even make false promises to get you to stay.

While they may sound convincing and while you may feel guilty about how you are making them feel, remind yourself that their reaction is not about losing you, it is about not being able to control you anymore. If you still love this person, they will be your weakness and you will probably feel horrible during this conversation, but remember that you are working on loving yourself more now and hold yourself accountable for this decision.

How do you think your partner will react? What can you do to prepare yourself?

_____

_____

_____

_____

_____

_____

_____

_____

_____

_____

_____

_____

_____

3. Soothe yourself

Let's say a child came to you feeling terrified and alone. They feel unsafe in the world and feel uncertain about what is going to happen to them, and they just need some reassurance to believe that they will be okay. You would probably empathize with the child and soothe their fears. You would do your best to make them see that things will not turn out so bad and that they can be safe. Even a few compassionate words can help this child feel more secure and less lonely. Now imagine that you are the child. The principle still applies – be compassionate about the pain you are feeling, because this is an excruciating situation. Tell yourself that although things seem scary now, you will get through this and you will be okay.

If you can get through this part of the process by soothing yourself, you can get through anything. If you have a support system you can rely on then they can help you through this too. However, you will be spending the most time with yourself and chances are you are going to need as much support as you can, so practice being your biggest supporter. Rely on yourself so that you build a tremendous amount of emotional strength to get through this difficult transition.

Your partner is incapable of processing their emotions in a healthy manner; they will not be able to rationalize why you are deciding to leave. Thus, it would be a waste of your time and energy to explain to them why you are leaving, because they will not take ownership of their part in the relationship and how badly they have treated you.

Emotional abusers believe they can do no wrong, so telling them that you are leaving because of their abuse will go into one ear and will come out the other. Instead, tell them that you have thought about this and you know that you deserve better. Stand firm. They will probably feel threatened to see you taking back your control, but do not let that waiver your stance. Love, encourage and soothe yourself, you can do this.

Write down some statements you can repeat to soothe yourself.

_____
_____
_____
_____
_____
_____
_____
_____
_____
_____

4. *Invest in YOU*

Be your own doctor and diagnose the emotional wounds you hold inside of you. It is difficult to do this without enough knowledge, so invest your time, energy and money (if needed) into hiring a life coach, a therapist or constantly watching tons of videos that can guide you on this journey of self-healing. Reading self-help books can help too! At this stage, there is no room for excuses. You might think you do not have the time, or that you do not have the money to do this, but think about what you want for your life. You will need to unlearn what you have been doing throughout your relationship and learn new healthy ways to redirect your mindset.

Investing in yourself will also give you the confidence to know that you will be okay. You will be giving yourself the tools you need to pull yourself out of a cycle and not repeat your mistakes. This will definitely feel scary, but it is a good kind of scary. By leaving the relationship, you have pushed yourself into the deep end of the pool; now invest in yourself so that it is easier for you to swim to the shallow end.

If you think about all the changes you need to make, it can feel overwhelming. Take it day by day and celebrate your progress. Each small win truly does add up to giving you a fantastic life and mindset. Constantly work on yourself and motivate yourself to do things for YOU. These things can include anything that makes you truly happy – hobbies, journaling, work, meeting new people, travelling, and so on. Invest in things you love. This will make your life feel much more fulfilling and you will realize that leaving your relationship was not such a bad idea. You will still have wounds from the relationship and that is inevitable, but the more you are aware of them and the more committed you are to work on yourself, the easier it will be to heal them.

What do you envision your dream life to be?

_____
_____
_____
_____
_____
_____
_____
_____
_____
_____

Make a list of things you can do/invest in to make your dream life a reality.

_____
_____
_____
_____
_____
_____
_____
_____
_____
_____
_____
_____
_____
_____

5. *Surround yourself with healthy people*

As you invest in and work on yourself, you will start to feel your energy become more positive and uplifting. At this point, let go of anybody who poisons your vibe and brings you down. There will be other toxic people you might know in your life, and as you are on this healing journey, if you recognize that there are certain people that do not serve your life's purpose anymore, you have every right to let them go. It will be painful, but it will ultimately make your life better.

Letting go of toxic people creates space for positive opportunities to come knocking at your door. Your energy attracts your network, so work on your vibe and you will start to see your network grow into a loving support system. Fill up your life with genuine and fantastic people, and it can only get better from there.

Who else in your life do you think drains your energy?

_____

_____

_____

_____

_____

_____

_____

_____

_____

_____

_____

_____

_____

_____

What kind of people do you want to attract in your life?

_____

_____

_____

_____

_____

_____

_____

_____

_____

_____

_____

_____

_____

_____

_____

_____

_____

_____

_____

_____

_____

Leaving an abusive relationship brings with it a whirlwind of mixed emotions. It is terrifying and it will not be easy. It may be the hardest thing you ever have to do, but the best things in life almost never come easily. Love yourself, build your confidence and prioritize your happiness. You've got this.

Chapter 16
How to forgive your partner when they have betrayed you

T hroughout your relationship, your partner must have done countless things to hurt you. Betrayal is not easy to get over – it is a
violation of your trust and once that trust is gone, it is an arduous process to win it back. Healthy relationships are built on trust, respect,
honesty and affection. Cheating, lying, stealing – these can all be cate-
gorized as betrayal. Abuse is also a form of betrayal, as they are violating
your trust to be safe. You have placed your trust in your partner to keep
you safe, happy and secure. You have trusted them to respect you and
treat you right. You have trusted them to be who they say they are and
not lie about their character. Emotional abuse breaks your trust in all
these areas and leaves you feeling deceived.

To many, it can seem impossible to forgive someone who has betrayed
them. Most people believe that if someone has done them wrong, they
do not deserve their forgiveness and forgiving them would mean letting
them off the hook. In all honesty, while that is the perception many
hold, it is not entirely accurate. Forgiveness actually has almost nothing
to do with the other person, it has to do with ourselves.

If you were to forgive someone for betraying you – let us take the example of a healthy person here – you would tell them that you forgive
them, but that does not do much for the other person. If they are able
to empathize, they would still feel guilt and shame for what they did to
you because they would know how it would have made you feel. Thus,
people do not really need your forgiveness in order to move on or feel
better. People move on with their lives on their own without your forgiveness, while you are still holding on to the anger and resentment you
feel towards this person for what they did to you. You are still carrying
around the negativity, and that can really do damage to your mental
health and energy. The other person probably does not think about

what they did to you as much as you do, so why give them that much importance?

At some point you will want to forgive your partner for the hurt they have caused you, but you may not know how to go about it and if it is even possible for you to do so. Therefore, here are some words of wisdom to keep in mind:

1. *Their act of betrayal had nothing to do with you*

Emotional abusers treat their victims badly because they have a void within themselves. It almost always has nothing to do with the other person. Remember, abusers are unable to deal with their insecurities and emotions in a healthy manner, and so they project them onto their partner using abusive tactics. They say nasty and hurtful things, and do everything they can to control your life so that they can feel superior. However, that is just it. They have a lack of self-worth within them, which is why they treat you as if you are lesser than, so that they can feel good about themselves. It is the coward's way out and realizing that will help you recognize that their betrayal does not have anything to do with the person you are or what you do or say.

Accepting that you are not the reason for their abuse is the first step. It is natural to take this personally, as you notice that your partner may not abuse anyone else as much as they do you. Or you might also take this personally simply because you are human, you are sensitive and it does ache when the person you love disrespects you like that. This can lead to you equating their abuse to you having low self-worth and self-value, but again, do not let someone else's words and actions dictate how amazing you are. You know your worth; you know what you bring to the table is irreplaceable and if your partner cannot handle that and tries to put you down, then that is on them, not you. Separate their actions from your sense of self-worth. The moment you accept that their betrayal is all about them, it will be easier to forgive.

This might be hard to believe right now, but you might even see the blessings in what happened to you later in life. Maybe being in an emotionally abusive relationship taught you so much about hardship, perseverance and growth, that you have become stronger than you ever have and will have an amazing life because of your strength now. Take the relationship as a lesson – what have you learned from it? Are there things you would never repeat? Are there things you think you did well? What did you learn about yourself? The painful experiences in life tend to be the most valuable lessons we learn. Do not rule out what the ups and downs of life can bring you – they might surprise you.

2. Forgiveness is continuous

Forgiveness is a process that continues over a period of time. It is rarely something you can do once and be done with. It is not easy to forgive someone and forget all about what happened. You may tell them that they are forgiven, but your wounds do not disappear overnight. It takes time for you to heal them and truly let go of what they did to you. You could be thinking about what happened often, you could be seeing your partner regularly and be reminded of what they did, or you could have conversations about it and be reminded that way too. Those wounds cannot just close up as soon as you decide to forgive someone. Keep in mind that if you do decide to forgive someone, that it will be a continuous process every time you see them or think about them until you have finally let go of all the anger, hurt and resentment.

3. Forgiveness gives you an opportunity to grow

A lot of the times, people do not forgive the person who betrayed them because their egos get in the way. Let's say, hypothetically, your partner cheated on you. That is an immensely huge act of betrayal a person could do in a relationship, and it would be devastating to endure for you. You would go through all that pain, process all your thoughts and emotions, struggle with trust issues, fight with your partner, and maybe eventually call off the relationship. At this point, you know that this person wronged you, and disrespected you to break your trust. Your ego tells you that this person wronged you and that they do not deserve your forgiveness. They did not think about how you would feel during the moments they betrayed you, so they do not deserve a moment of your thoughts as well. This applies to any form of betrayal, even emotional abuse.

While it is normal to think about forgiveness from the egotistical point of view, it is also important to remember that the ego can sometimes block you from introspection. You know you did not do anything wrong in the situation in order to be betrayed, but it does help to think about that period of time and reflect on what was going on inside of you. Was there anything you were doing to allow this to happen? Were you not enforcing your boundaries? Were you projecting anything? Did you give your partner the impression at any point that you would tolerate betrayal? This is not to say that whatever your partner did was justified due to what you were struggling with internally, but it is just good to know what emotional wounds you struggle with in general. Again, them betraying you is completely unacceptable and is on them.

Not every situation is black and white, and it is good practice to introspect nonetheless, so that you can rule out all the explanations. Be careful not to end up blaming yourself for what happened though – whatever they did speaks volumes about their character, no matter what was going on in the relationship. The only thing you need to reflect on is why your partner may have thought it was acceptable to do what they did and learn from it for next time. Betrayal is a bitter but inevitable lesson we learn in life, and it almost always makes us stronger in some aspect or another.

4. *Accept that you may not get an apology*

When someone has hurt you, common courtesy dictates that they apologize. It is a societal practice we abide by to ensure harmony and diplomacy in our relationships. Usually, most people understand this and feel remorse for what they have done. They empathize with what you might be feeling as a result of their betrayal and, at some point, ask you for forgiveness to relieve themselves of their guilt.

Toxic people, especially emotional abusers, do not have a huge empathy bone. Since they rarely accept that they are wrong, they will not feel guilt or shame because they will find a way to justify their betrayal, so that they do not have to go through the discomfort that comes with guilt or shame. If, by chance, they do apologize then that is great, but if they do not, try to accept that as gracefully as you can.

It is hard to accept – knowing that someone has clearly betrayed your trust and is not willing to take ownership for what they have done. Unfortunately, this is common nature for emotional abusers and sadly you cannot control how they behave. Even if they did apologize, it may not be sincere and would not mean anything to either of you. What you can control is how you react to their lack of remorse. You do not need their apology in order to move on from what happened.

What you need is self-love to heal. True forgiveness is when you have let go of the anger and resentment you hold towards this person and soothe the wounds they have left inside of you, regardless of whether they have apologized to you or not. Doing this does entail a roller coaster of emotions; you will have times when you question why this person deserves your forgiveness, but doing this is necessary for your peace of mind. It requires a lot of self-work and once you are on this journey of forgiveness, you will start to realize that it is necessary for your happiness, not theirs.

Forgive this person for yourself, not for their peace of mind. Once you truly let go of the negative feelings you have towards their betrayal, you begin to pull yourself out of the spiral of negativity and anger. Forgiveness removes the toxicity from your heart and leaves you with hope and positivity to move forward, and isn't that what life is all about?

What lessons have you learned about betrayal?

_____

_____

_____

_____

_____

_____

_____

_____

_____

_____

_____

_____

How has the experience of being betrayed changed you as a person?

_____

_____

_____

_____

_____

_____

_____

_____

_____

_____

_____

_____

When you introspect, what do you think made your part-
ner believe it was acceptable to betray you?

_____

_____

_____

_____

_____

_____

_____

_____

_____

_____

_____

Now focus on the present. What can you do to let go of this
experience and be happy again?

_____

_____

_____

_____

_____

_____

_____

_____

_____

_____

Chapter 17
Overcoming negative emotions

W hat exactly are negative emotions? They are the emotions that disrupt our peace of mind. Shame, anxiety, sadness, anger, guilt, jealousy, fear, and so on, are all otherwise known as "negative" emotions, because they can cause us discomfort, and even a tremendous amount of pain. Human beings have a tendency to run away from these feelings because they are too painful to endure. The general population seeks happiness and the minute they feel something coming that could interfere with that, they do everything in their power to hide from it.

Why do some people run away from negative emotions? These feelings challenge your state of mind and you might not know how to deal with it. Sometimes the feelings you have can be so overwhelming, that your mind tries to block them out in order to protect yourself. Some people, maybe due to culture, family values, society, etc., might believe that experiencing negative emotions and allowing them to be there is a sign of weakness. What people sometimes do not realize is that by pushing the feeling away, their mind is not actually eradicating it, but is simply suppressing it so that it can manifest in some other form.

If we dissect what emotions really are, we will not be as afraid of them. Emotions are just sensations in our body. You might feel sadness as heaviness behind the eyes or a lump in the throat. You might feel fear as a knot in your stomach or a rapid heartbeat. Each emotion brings with it a physical sensation that you can decipher.

Along with the physical sensations come the thoughts. What exactly are thoughts? They are a string of words that our mind is putting together. That is pretty much it - just a bunch words put together. Our mind has a funny way of coming up with the most absurd thoughts sometimes. What makes these thoughts so disturbing, is when we attach meaning and value to them. For example, you may have the thought that you will never be successful. If you look at that thought objectively, it is just a bunch of words strung together. However, your mind will start to attribute meaning to those words, eventually leading you to believe that there is truth to that statement. It then becomes a part of your belief system – that you will never be successful, and it was all based on a few words your mind conjured up based on assumptions, not facts.

This is what causes negative emotions – the stories we create in our heads. We come up with reasons as to why we should believe that thought based on assumptions, beliefs and insecurities. This fabrication of a story causes us so much pain that we push away the feeling altogether because we are scared there is truth to it.

In an emotionally abusive relationship, you experience a whirlwind of emotions regularly, but the most common ones are anxiety and extreme sadness (or heartache). Think about this scenario – a woman, let's call her Jane, is in a relationship with an emotional abuser, let's call him Henry. On a particularly difficult Wednesday, Jane has been working late in the office. She has to present to a new potential client the next day and everything needs to be perfect, as winning the business can mean a lot of money for the company and possibly a promotion for her too. Everything rides on this presentation. Due to the importance of this, she is not looking at her phone because her mind is focused on the presentation. Little does she know, Henry has called her and texted her multiple times asking where she is and why she is not responding. As she is almost done, she picks up her phone and sees Henry's missed calls. She immediately calls him back and apologizes for being MIA, and briefly explains that she was working and did not look at her phone.

She tells him she is coming home now and leaves the office. As soon as she opens the door to their house, Henry is waiting for her and starts yelling. He states that she does not love him or miss him enough to message him while she is working. He blames her for him messing up his dinner since he was so apprehensive. He guilts her into feeling like she does not deserve someone as good as him and that she should consider herself lucky that she has him. As Jane tries to calm him down and explain the situation, Henry gaslights her into thinking that her phone was intentionally switched off to avoid him. Jane, who obviously knows that this is not true, starts to second-guess herself because he is very convincing and has codependent tendencies. The fight ends with him saying that no other woman would do this and that he deserves better. He storms out of the house.

Jane's emotions are at an all-time high right now. She tries to call him multiple times on his phone, but his phone is switched off. Her anxiety is through the roof because she fears that he might do something out of revenge to hurt her, or he might leave her. She is hurt because he has said some awful things about her character. Due to his reaction, she also starts to feel guilty about focusing on her work and not responding to him on the phone. Jane is struggling to cope with her negative emotions right now and is experiencing a lot of heartache due to the way her partner, who she loves, has behaved with her.

Sadly, this is something that Jane goes through very regularly. Anxiety, heartache, shame, guilt, anger, and so on, are all emotions that she experiences almost every day because of her partner's abusive personality. She is so used to these negative emotions, that she experiences them even when her partner is not being abusive at that time. She fears setting him off and has to constantly think twice about everything she says or does. Since she is not fully secure with herself and fears being alone, she puts up with his behaviour and gives him what he demands. As a result, her mental health has deteriorated.

Situations like these are very common in emotionally abusive relationships, and anxiety and heartache become the two primary emotions a victim feels. You are probably familiar with the knot you get in your stomach or the rapid heartbeat you experience when you are dealing with an abuser. You might cry almost every day because of something your partner said or did, or you might be feeling extremely frustrated that no matter what you do, you are always wrong and you are unable to release your emotions. The anxiety and heartache you feel is enough to make you feel as though you are going crazy and you just want the abuse to stop. You want the abuse to stop but at the same time you feel powerless to do so. As a result, you are stuck with these negative emotions.

Your pain is understandable. It is not easy to deal with an emotional abuser while going through all these negative emotions. You may not be able to prevent the abuse or stop yourself from experiencing a negative emotion in the first place, but there are ways to cope with them if they do come around. To be able to overcome painful emotions, it is important to view the emotions and thoughts we have as sensations and words, because that is what they truly are. Your feelings are definitely valid and you are allowed to sit with them, but it is also important to remember that negative emotions are not harmful, in fact they are necessary for the human experience.

The best way to look at negative emotions is to perceive them as signals. They alert you when there is something going on inside of you that you need to address. Instead of fabricating stories in your head and upsetting yourself further, take the emotion and identify what is causing you to experience it. Dig deeper and peel the layers to find out why this particular feeling may have come about.

Unfortunately, when we were younger, we were not explicitly taught how to deal with our emotions most of the time. Society has taught us that we need to strive for happiness and any emotions other than that are inadmissible, when the fact of the matter is that negative emotions are just as welcome. Difficult and sad situations happen to us all the time, and you are allowed to experience the emotions that pop up. In order to be healthy, it is essential to allow the feelings to arrive. So, the next time you feel a negative emotion, make space for it to exist.

Acknowledge the signal and start to investigate why you are feeling this way. That is how you process emotions. The inner dialogue you have with yourself is the tool you need to be your own therapist. When you feel a negative emotion, look at it like a scientist. Be curious about it. Ask yourself questions about where it is coming from. The more questions you answer for yourself, the better you will understand and process your emotions. It is that easy. You will realize that the emotions you are feeling are not so scary after all, they were just ambiguous until you dissected them.

Self-love also helps you process your negative emotions. External situations will always present themselves, however it is up to you to recognize that you do deserve to be happy and therefore you need to understand why you feel the way you feel. Self-love will push you to introspect so that you can grow and accept everything about yourself.

What are the steps you need to take to process your negative emotions?

1. Manage your state of mind

As is constantly mentioned in this workbook, acknowledge how you feel and love yourself. Allow the emotion to exist within you and do not fight it. Do not fear the emotion and try to suppress it or numb yourself. Reassure your mind that it is okay to have this feeling and that it will not harm you. Being mindful of your emotions will be the first step to conquering peace for your state of mind.

2. Take ownership of your emotions

Once you recognize how you feel and allow your negative emotions to exist, take ownership for how you feel. There are external triggers that propel you into feeling a certain emotion and thinking a certain thought, but ultimately it is you who is choosing to feel a certain way and choosing how long you want to feel that emotion. Again, it is completely okay to feel what you feel for however long you need to, but if you find yourself revisiting that emotion over and over again, then you will stay stuck in it, which is a choice you are making. Own up to the choice you are making to feel that emotion, but then love yourself enough to work on letting go of it too. Take the time to introspect, understand why you are feeling this way, and relieve yourself of the strain.

3. Take the time to understand why you feel this way

As you sit with the feeling and create room for it, analyze it and figure out why you are experiencing it. It is easy to get stuck in the feeling because it might feel too heavy to investigate, and that is okay. Take your time, go easy on yourself. After you have had the chance to fully experience the emotion, pick yourself up and take a good look at what you are feeling. Ask yourself what has invoked these emotions within you. Examples of some questions you could ask are:

- When did I start feeling this way?
- Was there a particular trigger?
- What is the story I am telling myself?
- Have I fabricated this story or is it based on facts?
- Why does this situation bother me?
- Are there any emotional wounds I carry that might contribute to this situation and emotion?
- What do I need to happen in order to feel better about this situation?
- Why do I need that?

4. Change the story in your mind

As soon as you have identified the story behind your emotion, challenge it. Ask yourself if this story is based on your assumptions, insecurities and beliefs, or cold-hard facts. The validity of your story can still be intact due to your underlying emotional wounds, but the accuracy of it may be questionable. Take the time to assess it and see if there are any parts of the story that may solely be coming from deep within your vulnerable mind. Are you basing your emotions on past or future events? Doing this can also cause you to feel unnecessarily worse than you would want to. Focus on the present. List out the facts of the current situation and see how your emotions shift afterward.

Many times, we get so absorbed in what has happened to us in the past, or get overly anxious about what could happen in the future, that we overexert ourselves into feeling horrible, when in actuality there is no reason to feel so upset in the present. Ground yourself in the moment and recenter your emotions based on that. This way, you are able to remove yourself from the situation and process your emotions so that you can move forward to let them go.

5. *Look at your body language*

In addition to assessing your emotions and investigating the root cause, it helps to take a look at the current state of your body language too. Your body language can significantly determine how you feel. A slouched back, coupled with a frown and a tight jaw can put anybody on edge. If you notice yourself exhibiting any negative type of body language, change it. Stand up straight, unclench your jaw, loosen your frown and relax the muscles in your body. Interestingly, studies have shown that simply putting a smile on your face, even when you have no reason to smile, can uplift your mood. The muscles used to smile in your face signal to your brain that you are happy, so your mind starts to believe it and you actually do start feeling better. The same applies for when you are frowning – the muscles used to frown signal to your brain that you are frowning and as a result you start to feel crummier.
Observe your body language and see how you can best transition from that state to a more positive one. Even moving around and doing things helps! Walking, exercising, singing, dancing, cleaning, creating something, etc., are all great ways for you to take a break from the negative emotions and see that you can shift your focus to a better emotion. Once you create space for a positive emotion to exist, it makes it easier to welcome it and stay in that emotion as time goes on.

If your emotions were caused because of somebody else's actions or words, try having a rational conversation with them. It might be difficult to do this with an emotional abuser, but with a healthy person, this strategy still works. Conveying your thoughts and feelings in a constructive manner can invoke a healthy conversation between you two and aid in solving the matter, which in turn would help you resolve your negative emotions as well. If the person you are dealing with is toxic and does not take these kinds of conversations well, follow the steps above so that you feel as though you have some control over your emotions.

If you are used to fearing your emotions, be rest assured that there is nothing to fear now that you know these steps and have them handy in your wellness toolbox. Continue to have that inner dialogue with yourself when you have negative emotions and love yourself throughout. Life can be hard and scary, but parenting yourself can go a long way in helping you feel more secure. It all depends on what you say to yourself and how long you choose to stay in a certain emotional state. The next time you get a negative emotion, welcome it like an old friend. Remember, negative emotions are signals – like a text message alert, your emotions are alerting you to check the messages inside of you and address them. Do not fear your own emotions and thoughts – you will always be bigger than they are.

Practice processing your negative emotions:

1. ***What emotion are you feeling?***

_____

_____

_____

_____

_____

_____

_____

_____

_____

_____

2. **What are the sensations and thoughts you are experiencing?**

_____

_____

_____

_____

_____

_____

_____

_____

_____

_____

3. **What triggered this emotion?**

_____

_____

_____

_____

_____

_____

_____

_____

_____

_____

_____

4. **How long have you been feeling this for?**

_____
_____
_____
_____
_____
_____
_____
_____
_____
_____
_____

5. **What is the story you are associating with this situation and emotion?**

_____
_____
_____
_____
_____
_____
_____
_____
_____
_____

6. **How much of the story is based on facts vs. assumptions? Write them all down.**

Facts:

_____

_____

_____

_____

_____

_____

_____

_____

_____

_____

_____

Assumptions:

_____

_____

_____

_____

_____

_____

_____

_____

_____

_____

_____

7. *What emotional wounds may be contributing to the intensity of this feeling?*

_____
_____
_____
_____
_____
_____
_____
_____
_____
_____
_____

8. *Are you basing your emotions on the past or the future? Explain.*

_____
_____
_____
_____
_____
_____
_____
_____
_____
_____
_____

9. *How can you change the story to reflect what is true in the present?*

_____

_____

_____

_____

_____

_____

_____

_____

_____

_____

_____

10. *What is your current body language? How can you change it?*

_____

_____

_____

_____

_____

_____

_____

_____

_____

_____

_____

11. **What activities can you do to shift your emotional state from a negative one to a positive one?**

_____

_____

_____

_____

_____

_____

_____

_____

_____

_____

_____

_____

_____

_____

_____

_____

_____

_____

_____

Good job! You successfully assessed your emotions, reframed the story you are telling yourself and planned what you can do to help yourself feel a little better. The more you do this, the more automatic this strategy will become. Soon enough, you will be a master of coping with negative emotions!

Chapter 18
How to get your power back after a break-up

B reak-ups are rarely easy. If you were invested in the relationship and had deep feelings for the other person, you would feel immense pain from letting that person go. You would have shared so many experiences together, good and bad. Having a deep and emotional connection with someone is beautiful, but it also makes it that much harder to let go of them should the relationship not work out. It can feel as though all that time, energy and love you invested into the other person was all for nothing, since you did not reach your "happily ever after" with them. If your relationship was relatively healthy, you would most likely think about all the great times you had with this person and wish things were different. It is natural to feel this way – you had a great connection and you loved them. If your relationship was emotionally abusive, you would probably be dealing with heartbreak as well as some deep emotional wounds from the abuse you endured.

A break-up is a form of loss. You are losing the romantic connection you had with that person and it is completely normal to grieve that loss. Much like any tragedy, you will most probably go through the five stages of grief during your break-up.

What are the five stages of grief during a break-up?

1. *Denial*

The first stage of grief entails you not being able to accept that you and your partner have broken up. The rational side of your brain may have acknowledged the break-up, but your emotional side takes over and protects you from the pain you would feel if you actually absorbed the break-up. Denial is a coping mechanism that "softens" the initial shock of the loss, in which your mind tends to ignore the reality of the situation and chooses to believe that there must be another explanation. You might not be willing to accept that your bond with this person has changed and that you probably will not have the same relationship with them again. Losing them will feel like a deep loss.

2. Anger

Once you have accepted that the relationship is over, you may find yourself feeling angry a lot of the time. The emotions that were previously numbed by denial start to come back to the surface and the huge wave of emotional turmoil manifests in anger. Your anger can be projected onto inanimate objects, people outside of the relationship, or your ex-partner for their role in the demise of the relationship and you may start to resent them. You may even direct some anger towards yourself if you think you did not do enough for the relationship and feel some amount of shame. If you left an emotionally abusive relationship, chances are you will feel angry when you reflect on all the abuse your partner directed towards you, and resent them for their actions, as well as yourself a little bit for tolerating it. Again, it is important to remember that you did not know back then what you know now, and to cut yourself some slack.

3. Negotiation

This is when you feel most vulnerable and helpless but are still fighting to gain comfort by negotiating. You have accepted that the break-up has happened but still want to gain control over the situation.

You might think of what-if scenarios about the relationship and wonder if things would have been different, or you might bargain with a spiritual entity you deem powerful to give you back the relationship in exchange for anything.

This is when you think about all the good things the relationship had to offer, even if it had more negatives than positives, and as a result your emotions drive you to bargain for relief.

4. Depression

This is the phase where you feel hopeless. You have done everything you can and now it has finally sunk in that this relationship is over. Sadness and grief set in and this is when you might isolate yourself from social events or you may lose interest in doing things that once brought you pleasure. This is when you start to process the loss and begin to accept the separation. At this point in time, all you really need is a hug and a shoulder to cry on.

5. Acceptance

The final, and possibly the most long awaited, stage is acceptance. This is when the pain you feel inside of you starts to get less intense as the days go by. You feel calmer and are able to function in daily life. Acceptance is not to be confused with happiness – happiness takes its time and many people try to rush the grieving process to get to the happiness phase. Acceptance happens when you finally absorb the reality of the situation while still moving forward with your life. You start to believe that you can find love again and that you will be okay; that this is not the end of your life. You start to socialize again and do things to help yourself feel more alive.

Most people go through these five stages of grief during a break-up, but it is common for some people to skip a stage or two or experience them simultaneously. It differs from person to person. There is no cookie-cutter manual on how to heal from a break-up, since everybody's situations vary. However, there is hope to moving on, no matter how long it takes.

Being in a relationship sometimes results in you losing yourself a little bit to the other person. Sacrifice and compromises cause you to forget certain aspects of who you are in order to make the relationship work. That is normal in most healthy relationships, as long as it does not turn into codependency and insecurity.

However, in an emotionally abusive relationship, your partner was controlling you and so you might have left the relationship forgetting who you are. You might be so used to them dictating your life that you realize that you have not exercised the "leadership" muscle in your own life. You could be confused and scared to lead this new life of yours without consulting the other person. Because of all the abuse you endured, you might not know what is deemed normal and what is deemed unhealthy, and navigating through these murky waters alone can be overwhelming, especially when you have not reconnected with yourself and do not know who you truly are.

So, how do you gain control over your life and get your power back after a break-up?

1. *Be patient with yourself*

Break-ups are hard and are one of the most excruciatingly painful things to go through. You will feel negative emotions and, at times, it will feel so burdensome that you may have trouble coping. After all, your mind and body are not used to being without this person, and so you will face the withdrawal symptoms. Remember, this is all normal when you are going through a break-up and you need to be patient with yourself. Give yourself time to grieve the loss of the relationship – that goes for emotionally abusive ones too. It will take time to process the loss and to keep your head above water, so make sure you do not pressure yourself to rush through the pain. The negative emotions may shatter you to your core, but it is necessary for you to go through this pain so that you can come out through to the other side feeling stronger. As mentioned earlier, negative emotions are part of the human experience and are necessary for you to move forward to a better life. Instead of fearing them, face them.

Expecting yourself to immediately be happy after a break-up is unrealistic and an injustice to yourself, because you are assuming you will not be able to deal with the pain. You most certainly can, you have the strength within you, you just need to realize you have it and that it takes time to heal. You may have the thought that this pain is going to last forever and that you will never be free from it, however keep reminding yourself that after being so invested in a relationship, it takes time and practice to recalibrate yourself and work towards feeling content.

Coming out of an emotionally abusive relationship means that you will probably experience symptoms of depression, anxiety, anger and insecurity due to all the abuse you were put through. It will be a difficult journey towards healing, but it is not impossible. You need to be mindful of the story you are telling yourself. If you are telling yourself the story that you will not be able to cope, you will never find love again and that you are not worth it, simply acknowledge that your mind is feeding you a negative story and that it is just a bunch of words. If you get lost in that story, you will start to believe that the story is true and that it is unchangeable, which is definitely not the case. Remember, just because a certain negative thought comes into your head, does not mean that it holds any value. Observe it, assess whether there is truth to it, let it go and then tell yourself a more realistic and hopeful story. You are in control of what you feed your mind and what you want to believe. The more mindful you are of your stories, the easier it will be to pull yourself out of negative spirals during this break-up.

In addition to being patient with yourself, be patient with those around you as well. If you are getting out of an emotionally abusive relationship, chances are a few of your friends and family members will speak their minds about what the relationship was like and will pressure you to move on quickly. They will probably ask you why you are still in love with the person, or ask you why you are taking so long to get over them. It is easy to get stuck in the perceived judgment that you feel coming from these people and you might feel frustrated with their insensitivity, but just remember that they are coming from a place of love and that they do not understand what you are going through.

Not everybody experiences what it is like to be in an emotionally abusive relationship, and so they may not fully understand why you are taking the time you need. Take whatever they say with a pinch of salt and remind yourself that they just want the best for you and are rooting for you to be happy. Monitor the conversations you have with people and be mindful of where they are coming from, because chances are, they are not saying what they are saying with malicious intent. You know what you went through in this relationship, so you are entitled to dictate how and for how long you process this break-up and move on.

2. *Focus on rebuilding your life*

After being in a shared codependent life with an abuser, it is completely normal and understandable to fear starting over. It is scary to think about all the endless possibilities you have now and you may find all the options overwhelming and will not know which path to choose. You might even second-guess your ability to focus on yourself, but then again that is a story that you are choosing to believe. You can either choose to envision the story of not being able to do this, or the story of you rising to the occasion and getting back control of your life. Do you want to tell yourself the scary story or the hopeful one? The decision is yours.

Going for the hopeful story means that you have to reassess where your life is currently, then envision where you want your life to be. Which areas of your life need some work? There are six areas of your life that shape who you are (some life coaches use slightly different models, but the premise is usually the same):

1. *Finances*

The amount of earnings you have to sustain your current life, as well as support the life you hope to have in the future based on your cash flow, investments, assets and any liabilities you may have accumulated.

2. *Personal growth*

The constant work you do on yourself to realize your full potential based on your dreams, values, beliefs and maturity.

3. *Social life*

Your network of friends who you spend time with and share experiences with. This area of your life focuses on the interpersonal bonds that you form with other people and how you nurture them.

4. *Romantic relationships*

Refers to the intentional bond you form with another person who you aim to share most of your life experiences with. The goal is usually to find somebody who will be a significant part of your present and future.

5. *Family*

The people you love, take care of and are a part of your home life. Your family is the group of people that love you unconditionally through thick and thin.

6. *Career*

Your professional life which includes your education, training and work experiences. This is the area of your life where you choose a specialized trade and make a living out of it.

When you go through a break-up, the romantic relationship aspect of your life will certainly be affected and that is the area you may focus on while you heal. Although it is natural for you to want to find someone better, doing it while you are still healing from your past relationship, especially an abusive one, makes you negate the other areas of your life. Most of the time, there will be a few areas in your life that might need some more attention, apart from the romantic relationship area. For example, your career might be going great as you might have found your calling, but your finances may not be where you would want them to be, as you might be unable to save as much money as you would like. In this scenario, you would focus your attention on other options that would allow you to earn more or cut costs. Going through a break-up is devastating, but the good news is that it gives you the opportunity and time to evaluate where you want your life to be, and assess which areas need more work in order for you to get there.

Working on the areas in your life that are lagging behind gives you a sense of hope. As you take the steps to make those areas better, you will start to realize that you have gained back control over your life and that there is hope for a more fulfilling future. If you do not take action to make those areas better for yourself, you might fall into the victim role and feel depressed about not moving forward. The truth is, it is all in your hands, you just need to take the first step.

As for the romantic relationship area of your life, that will develop at some point too. After coming out of an emotionally abusive relationship, the priority is to focus on loving yourself and feeling fulfilled without validation from another person. You may have been extremely codependent in your last relationship, and if you go into a new one with that same sense of lacking, you will constantly expect your new partner to fill your glass. As you know, this can cause emotional strain on the relationship and your expectations may never be met. Instead, when you work on the other areas of your life, you start to recognize that life consists of many other things that can make you happy, not just a relationship. You start to believe that life has so much more to offer and you even become more confident because you have worked on all of these areas on your own. Nothing can bring you down now.

As you keep working on your life, your vibration changes to a more hopeful and positive one, your glass will start to fill up, which means that you will start attracting potential partners that are healthy and deserving of you. You will start to make smarter choices about who you let into your life and this will show you that you deserve the best. You will not need anybody to fill your glass anymore because you will have filled it yourself with all these other amazing things that you are doing. The new partner you attract will just add more value to your life. Thus, focus on the other aspects of your life and get excited about bettering those, because you want to be ready for that amazing person to come into your life when you are at your most confident and highest vibration.

3. Practice setting boundaries

This is a recurring theme in the workbook because it is so important. If you were in an emotionally abusive relationship, you are probably used to your boundaries being ignored and your partner disrespecting you. Now that you are out of that relationship, things can change.

Think back to the relationship and identify what you were willing to tolerate, even though it went against what you wanted or believed in. Once you have identified those, set your boundaries in your mind. Reiterate to yourself that these are the things that you are not willing to compromise on and that if someone ignores your boundary, then you will not tolerate it.

Raise the standards of how you want to be treated, because you are in control of how you allow people to treat you. Whoever you deal with in your life moving forward, communicate your boundaries to them and strictly enforce them. If they are emotionally healthy, they will respect your standards. If they are toxic, chances are they will not respect them in the first couple of tries.

No matter how much a person defies your boundaries, be strong and continue to enforce them. The more you do this, the easier it will get for you. If the person still does not respect your standards, then you need to think about whether or not you need to distance yourself from them.

When you enforce your boundaries, people know you mean business and actually respect you for standing up for yourself. As you keep working on yourself and loving yourself, enforcing those boundaries will get easier and easier the more you practice. At some point, you will be enforcing those standards from a place of confidence, not from a place of lacking.

4. *Forgiveness*

Learn to forgive yourself. There will be times when you look back at the relationship and want to kick yourself in the head for staying in it for as long as you did, and for tolerating as much as you did too. Self-criticism during this time may be at an all-time high because you will think that you should have done things differently, but it is important to remember that the person you were during that relationship was not aware of exactly what abuse is. You were trying your best at that time and you might not have been confident enough to believe that you would be okay if you left your partner at that time. That version of yourself was still you, and self-love involves accepting each version of yourself regardless of the weaknesses you have. What is important is that you learn from that version of yourself and ensure that you do not repeat the same mistakes moving forward.

Empathy, confidence, validation and compassion are going to be the most important tools you need to sharpen during this time, because they will help bring you out of any negative spirals you may fall into. Do not be so harsh on yourself. The fact that you are even reading this book shows that you want better for yourself and that you want to heal. Give yourself some credit. If a person you love came to you and started criticizing themselves for what they endured in their relationship, you would most likely talk to them from an angle of compassion and empower them to focus on the present and be hopeful for improvement in the future. If you can do that for someone else, you can definitely do that for yourself. You will be your biggest cheerleader. Forgive yourself for tolerating that abusive relationship, and look forward to better times ahead.

Additionally, if you are at a healthy point in your life, you can try to forgive your partner for what they did to you as well. Not for them, but for yourself. The abuse your partner put you through was completely unacceptable; there are no excuses to justify how they treated you. What you need to realize is that your ex-partner was unhealthy. They did not and probably will not ever recognize that what they did to you was completely inappropriate. Since you may never see their remorse, it can help you to move forward if you mentally forgave them for what they did, so that you can let go of the negativity and toxicity you may carry because of their actions. Forgiveness is more about your peace of mind, rather than "letting them off the hook". Once you forgive them, you will start to feel a weight lift from your shoulders, because you can finally start to remove their importance from your life and focus on better people.

5. *Educate yourself on self-love*

Learning more about emotional abuse can never hurt. By now you know what the warning signs are, what abusive tactics a toxic person uses and how to get out of abusive situations. While educating yourself on emotional abuse is necessary, make sure it does not turn into an obsession. Reflect on your emotionally abusive relationship, pin-point what aspects were unacceptable and make a mental note of them.

What you should be prioritizing is learning how to love yourself. You have been in a relationship that has not given you the love you deserve, so now it is time to make up for it. If you need to watch instructional videos, read books, consult life coaches or therapists, do it. Do whatever you need to gain the strength, motivation and tools needed to shower yourself with love. You are an amazing person and you deserve all the love you want. Gift yourself the knowledge on how to love yourself.

Your journey during this break-up is most likely not going to be linear. Like an addiction, you may have relapses and withdrawal symptoms. Healing will feel like an emotional roller coaster that you cannot get off, but keep pushing through because the ride will calm down and come to a halt if you persevere. Reflect on your relationship, be patient, set your boundaries, forgive, educate and love yourself. Sooner or later, you will move on and life will look much rosier.

If you are grieving your break-up, what stage of the grieving process do you think you are in and why?

_____

_____

_____

_____

_____

_____

_____

_____

_____

_____

_____

How can you remind yourself to be more patient while healing?

_____

_____

_____

_____

_____

_____

_____

_____

_____

_____

_____

What do you want your life to look like moving forward?

_____
_____
_____
_____
_____
_____
_____
_____
_____
_____
_____
_____
_____

What areas of your life are doing well? Which areas need improvement?

Areas doing well and why:

_____
_____
_____
_____
_____
_____
_____
_____

Areas that need improvement and why:

_____

_____

_____

_____

_____

_____

_____

_____

_____

_____

_____

What steps can you take to improve the areas in your life that need more work?

_____

_____

_____

_____

_____

_____

_____

_____

_____

_____

_____

_____

What boundaries do you want to set moving forward? What would the consequences be if someone crossed the line?

_____
_____
_____
_____
_____
_____
_____
_____
_____
_____
_____
_____

What can you tell yourself to help you forgive your ex-partner and yourself?

_____
_____
_____
_____
_____
_____
_____
_____
_____
_____
_____

How will you educate yourself on emotional abuse and self-love?

_____

_____

_____

_____

_____

_____

_____

_____

_____

_____

_____

_____

_____

_____

_____

_____

_____

_____

_____

_____

_____

_____

_____

_____

_____

_____

_____

Chapter 19
Self-love habits

A s mentioned, multiple times in this workbook, self-love is the biggest key to healing from your emotionally abusive relationship. Self-love is the appreciation for who you are at this moment in time. It is influenced by how you talk to yourself, how you view yourself, and the things you do for yourself. It is heavily determined by your attitude and treatment towards YOU.

Your perception of yourself plus the emotional wounds inflicted on you by your ex-partner have a big effect on how worthy you think you are of love. If you have low self-esteem and were in a relationship with an emotional abuser, your partner (or ex-partner) would have manipulated you into thinking that you are undeserving of love and that you were lucky to have them because they would be the only ones who would love you.

Sadly, you might have believed them. Abusers usually say this so that you believe you will not find anyone else and, as a result, will stay in the relationship no matter what. This, along with the other cruel and abusive tactics, make you doubt your self-worth and leave wounds that cut deep. These wounds are usually still open and prevent you from actually seeing how amazing you are, because you have been fed the information that you are not special.

So, how do you start to love yourself again?

1. *Be grateful*

As cliché as it sounds, being grateful really does help you on your journey to self-love. Your life may have its ups and downs, and there may be areas that you are extremely unhappy with, but chances are you do have some areas that are going really great for you too. Even if it is something as simple as you having clothes on your back and having clean drinking water. Those are still things to be grateful for because those things do not come easily to everybody. If you constantly focus on the negative aspects of your life, you will miss out on the beauty that your life is offering you.

Of course, like everybody else, you do strive to get what you want and you do have a plan to get to where you want to, however life does not always go according to plan. Sometimes the good things you want in life take longer than expected, either because it is not the right time yet or there is something better in store. It is important to realize that none of us have total control over what life throws at us, so as we work hard on the areas of our lives that need improvement, it is essential to recognize the areas that are already doing well in the meantime. Chances are, you probably have something going for you in your life that someone else is wishing for.

Gratitude is powerful because even if your life is not where you want it to be, it shifts your focus to what you do have. As a result, you start to feel more positive and confident about where your life is heading. When you think about what you lack, your mindset tends to get stuck in the victim role and starts to believe that nothing will work out. The best way to relieve catastrophic thinking is to prove to yourself that your life does have some magic in it already. You will still work hard to achieve what you want in life, but you will do it from a place of love and happiness, not from a place of lack.

The grass may always look greener on the other side, but why allow yourself to be bothered by the other side? Focus on watering and nurturing your own side so that it looks the greenest it can ever be. Try maintaining a gratitude journal and write down 3 things you are grateful for every day. It does not matter how big or small each point is, all that matters is that you recognize the blessings you have. Writing this down every day will make it feel real and you will actually start to believe that your life is pretty great at this moment!

What are 3 things you are grateful for today? (Do this every day)

_____

_____

_____

_____

2. Be mindful of your thoughts

Our minds bring out thousands of thoughts a day, and some of these can be irrational. This is completely normal. However, you might find yourself feeling anxious, depressed, guilty, shameful, angry, disgusted or any other negative emotion because of a thought. Why does this happen? It happens because you are getting stuck in that thought that is causing that emotion. For example, if you have the thought "I am not good-looking enough" and you keep ruminating on it, you could spiral from there and start thinking even more irrational thoughts such as "I am not going to find love" or "nobody thinks I am desirable". From there, you will start to feel sad, anxious and your confidence in yourself will drop to the ground. All because of one single thought that you decided to attach yourself to.

Instead, try to observe your thoughts from afar. Be mindful of what types of thoughts come into your head and if it is worth getting stuck on. If the "I am not good-looking enough" thought pops up, remind yourself that no good can come from engaging with it and try to let it pass by. Your thoughts are not the sole truth of life – they are just a bunch of words strung along together. The minute you get stuck on them and hold value to them, that is when you perceive them to be the truth. You are in control of which thoughts you want to entertain, and which thoughts are not worth your energy.

Pro tip: picture your thoughts as clouds passing by – it really helps! It distances you from the thought and allows you to view them as harmless entities that will eventually pass. If you are not a fan of picturing clouds, you could picture them as waves, cars on the street, leaves, whatever works for you!

Keep a thought journal. What thoughts are you having, and are they helpful or harmful? Why? Write some down here.

_____

_____

_____

_____

_____

_____

_____

_____

_____

_____

_____

_____

_____

_____

_____

_____

_____

_____

_____

_____

_____

_____

_____

3. Minimize self-criticism

You are human. You have great strengths that add to your uniqueness, but you also struggle with a few things, which is okay! It is actually necessary for you to struggle in order to develop your character and grow from it. Sometimes, however, your mind might perceive your struggles to be "flaws" and criticize you for having them. Your inner critic shines the spotlight on your "flaws" and blocks out all the great things about you. This happens when you have an unrealistic standard you need to meet for yourself, and anything less than that is unacceptable. Even if you did meet that standard, you would probably still find a fault within you. For example, if you were aiming to finish an 80,000-word dissertation within two months but instead it took you two and a half months, your inner critic would focus on the fact that it took you fifteen more days to finish it, not that you actually achieved something monumental.

It is completely acceptable and healthy to aim high and work to attain your goals. However, you need to remember that you are doing your best and that you are still a shining star, even if you do not quite meet your goals exactly as planned. Constantly honing in on what you think you lack within you will reduce your self-confidence. If you are a loving person, you probably would not criticize your friend or family member this much, so why do it to yourself?

You will probably have emotional wounds from your past, even from your abusive relationship, and these will feed your inner critic, but the healthy thing to do is to simply acknowledge the criticism, and then make a decision on how to perceive it. You can either believe what your inner critic says and feel horrible about yourself, or you can choose to reframe that piece of criticism to inspire you to work hard, while illuminating your good qualities. Give yourself compliments and positive affirmation, so that even when your inner critic starts to run their mouth again, you know deep down that for all the qualities you may need work on, you also have an abundance of qualities that are absolutely amazing.

What do you usually criticize yourself for?

_____
_____
_____
_____
_____
_____
_____
_____
_____
_____

*Now change those criticisms to constructive statements
that will uplift you, rather than bring you down.*

_____
_____
_____
_____
_____
_____
_____
_____
_____
_____
_____
_____
_____
_____

Write down 50 positive affirmations for yourself.

4. *Monitor how you talk to yourself*

Similar to your inner critic, your inner dialogue determines how you perceive yourself. The way you talk to yourself can greatly influence your mental health. If you choose to say negative things about the world and yourself, you will start to feel negative emotions which, if they go unchecked, can result in anxiety and depression. What people forget is that we have the power to control the conversations we have with ourselves. Next time you feel yourself getting stressed by your thoughts, take a step back and observe what you are telling yourself. Essentially, you need to tell yourself to chill out a little bit, and not be so hard on yourself.

Again, it is easy to get caught in negative self-talk, but it is not necessary because it is not the truth. Practice changing the way you talk to yourself – make the conversation more positive, enlightening and encouraging. Giving yourself positive affirmations can help you feel better about yourself and will make your inner dialogue more helpful than harmful. If you have been in an emotionally abusive relationship, chances are you need this more than anybody. You were possibly put down more than you were lifted up, and somewhere along the way you stayed down. Now is your chance to lift yourself up again by talking to yourself with great care and love.

Give yourself the validation that you seek. If you constantly look for validation from other people, you will always feel empty. There is only so much another person can tell you to make you feel loved. You have to tell yourself the positive things you want to hear and reassure yourself. Your validation will guide you to truly believing that you are a beautiful person. If you have trouble with this, try journaling. Write down how you feel and the conversations you have with yourself on a daily basis. After you have written them down, re-read what you have written and identify any areas where you might be a little too pessimistic, or a little too hard on yourself. Once identified, change the words and phrases to be a little more realistic and encouraging. The more you practice this, the easier it will get.

What conversations do you usually have with yourself?
What are the topics? Are you usually pessimistic or hope-
ful?

_____

_____

_____

_____

_____

_____

Write down some examples of negative statements you usu-
ally say about yourself or about the world.

_____

_____

_____

_____

_____

_____

Now change those statements to be more realistic and help-
ful. Repeat those to yourself 3 times and observe how it
makes you feel.

_____

_____

_____

_____

_____

_____

5. *Take care of your physical health*

Your physical health has a huge influence on your mental health. There are countless studies that show how your diet and exercise regime contribute to how you feel mentally. Eating nutritious food balances your body's minerals and vitamins, which in turn help your brain to function a little better. If you eat a lot of fast food and sugar, chances are your body is deprived of the essential nutrients it needs and is replacing them with processed and unhealthy food. As a result, your body is running on the wrong nutrients and you start to feel more lethargic, angry, upset and anxious. Make small changes to your meals to ensure you have incorporated all the necessary areas of the food pyramid. That way, your balanced diet can translate to a balanced mind too.

Doing some physical exercise helps your mind feel better too. You do not have to do a high-intensity workout every day; simply getting up and going for a walk is good enough too. As long as your body is moving, the "feel-good" hormones called endorphins are released into your bloodstream and make you feel much better.

Additionally, start making a note of the unhealthy habits you have and change them. Are there any healthier, more helpful habits you can start to adopt? If you smoke cigarettes, could you maybe cut down on the number of times you smoke in a day or week? If you love to eat fast food often, can you reduce the quantity and frequency of doing that?

If you want to get really serious about it, keeping a habit journal helps you keep track of the changes you want to make. Write down what your goals are first. If you want to exercise more often, write that down as your goal. Next, come up with habits you can adopt to ensure that you meet this goal. For example, one habit can be walking outside twice a week. Another one could be doing some high-intensity cardio workouts twice a week. As the days go by, cross off each day in which you successfully stuck to your healthy habit and write down how it made you feel. There are various habit tracker templates online you can find to help you with this.

When you start to take care of your body, you begin to feel more confident about yourself and you start to love yourself for who you are. You genuinely start to believe that your mind and body are temples that you need to take care of, and you will ensure that you keep doing just that.

What are some unhealthy habits you want to get rid of?

_____

_____

_____

_____

_____

_____

_____

_____

_____

_____

What are some healthy habits you want to adopt?

_____

_____

_____

_____

_____

_____

_____

_____

_____

_____

6. *Step out of your comfort zone*

Another essential part of self-love is enhancing your personal development. If you want to feel better and do better in your life, you will need to change it up a little by stepping out of your comfort zone. The areas in your life that need improvement will not progress if you keep doing the same things you have always been doing. You do not have to make monumental changes; even tiny changes will add up to the result you seek – as long as you are consistent. Consistency is key to growing.

For example, if your social life is not where you would like it to be, think of ways you can step out of your comfort zone. You could make sure you talk to someone new if you go to a social event, or you could put your phone away when you are having a conversation with someone and give them your full attention. When you start seeing the results of your minor changes, you will get a huge confidence boost and will start to love getting out of your comfort zone. Nudge yourself out of the comfort zone and you will feel extremely proud of yourself, and that is the validation you need.

In what areas of your life do you want to grow?

_____

_____

_____

_____

_____

_____

_____

_____

_____

_____

What are some things you can do to step out of your comfort zone to achieve this personal growth?

_____

_____

_____

_____

_____

_____

_____

_____

_____

_____

_____

_____

7. Quit comparing yourself to other people

It is natural to start comparing ourselves to other people; after all, we live in an integrated society and technology makes it easy to know about the depths of someone's life. However, comparison is the opposite of self-love. Instead of focusing on believing that you are a stellar human being, you are focusing on other people's lives and putting yourself down because some areas of your life may not match up to theirs. However, it is important to remember that everyone has their own journey. There is no set rulebook in life that dictates what a "perfect life" looks like and what should be the timeline of everybody's achievements. You could have a wonderful life, but because you are looking at somebody else's life that may be different than yours, you might start to feel a sense of lacking, when in actuality it is just different. Your perception of your own life gets distorted due to someone else's journey.

One big contributor to the demon of comparison is social media. While it is a fantastic way to stay updated on your social network's lives, stay abreast with current world news and keep in touch with old friends, it is also guilty of portraying false perfection. Your social circle will rarely update their social media with what they are struggling with, but they will most likely update it with a photo layered with filters to make themselves feel good. While this is completely fine, you need to remember that just because someone looks like they are having the time of their life, does not mean that they do not have their own struggles as well. This distorted image of other people's lives is what causes our downfall and it is essential to remember that there is a much more complex story off-screen.

It is easier said than done, but practice being content with your own life in the present moment. Your journey has its own beauty too and the more you focus on your personal growth, the rosier your life will start to look. There is no one else like you in the world who has had the same life experiences, personality traits, physical features, social circle, and so on. You are unique – so it does not make sense to compare yourself to another person, because you both are still very different people with different lives. Remember, everyone is human. Everybody is thriving and struggling in various areas of their life, just like you.

Who have you compared yourself to and why? How did that make you feel?

_____
_____
_____
_____
_____
_____
_____
_____

Write down 10 things about your own life that are pretty great.

_____

_____

_____

_____

_____

_____

_____

_____

_____

_____

_____

_____

_____

8. Do things you love

As you work on reframing your thoughts and taking care of your physical health, engage in activities that you love as well. This could be anything – whatever it is that makes you feel genuinely happy and fulfilled. For some reason, human beings love to take the time to find all the things that are not going well for them. They can spend hours coming up with reasons as to why they are not good enough or why they should not take the leap in doing something they have wanted to do for a long time. Imagine if everybody would allocate that time instead to actually do things that they love. Wouldn't that be time well-spent?

Think of all the things you said you would do. It could be learning how to cook a new recipe, or it could be starting a musical project. It could even be something as simple as going outside for a walk in the park every couple of days. If it makes you happy, then do it. Doing the things you love will fill you up with happiness because you will not feel pressured to do these things out of obligation, you will be motivating yourself to do them because it is your decision. Consequentially, you will start to feel more confident about yourself and love yourself because the happiness you gain from doing these activities will make you feel like a new person. You will start to love your daily routine. Do things for yourself, you deserve it.

Write down some things you love to do and how often you aim to do them from now on.

_____

_____

_____

_____

_____

_____

_____

_____

_____

_____

_____

_____

_____

If your daily life is a little hectic right now and you do not feel like you have the time to practice these self-love tactics, try to reframe how you think about this. You would not neglect brushing your teeth in the morning, no matter how little time you have, because it is important and is a priority. The same applies for self-love and care, make yourself a priority, even if it is just for 15 minutes a day. Those 15 minutes will help you reconnect with yourself and make you feel on top of the world. Focus on your growth, recognize your insecurities, parent yourself throughout the process and start to change the way you see your life.

Conclusion

C ongratulations! You have completed the workbook and have gained so much knowledge throughout the process. You may have started this workbook as a completely different person, and the more you read along and did the exercises, the more you started to self-reflect and grow. Even if you feel like you grew only just a little, that is still amazing! Completing this workbook is the first step in your personal development. You carved out time to learn about emotional abuse and you were brave enough to think back on your own relationship to identify the abuse. That takes a lot of strength and you should definitely be proud of yourself. It is not an easy feat to accomplish.

The knowledge you have gained in this workbook will serve as your intelligence in the future should you have to deal with emotional abuse ever again. You will easily recognize what abuse is and there will be no room for confusion. Of course, do not diagnose everybody who has an unfavourable quality as an emotional abuser. Make sure you look at the person as a whole and evaluate them properly so that you can correctly determine whether they have your best interest at heart. You have the information, now just apply it in real life – whether you do this with your current partner or somebody else in your life who you think may be an abuser, make use of the information available to you.

This workbook has also taught you the best strategies to handle an emotionally abusive person, and when it is best to let go of that connection with them. By doing the exercises in this workbook, you have gotten accustomed to reflection and this skill will prove extremely useful to you whenever you are dealing with a toxic person. The strategies you have learned will also be important tools in your emotional toolbox, just remember to practice using them. The more you use them, the easier and more automatic this will become for you.

The strongest tool you have learned and will need to keep learning about is self-love. The exercises in this book have helped you to introspect on your insecurities and soothe yourself so that you can accept them and work on healing them. It is so important to love yourself for who you are, because only then will you see your own worth. Love is a powerful vibration and if you are able to truly love yourself, then your vibe attracts some amazing opportunities into your life. When you focus on growing each aspect of your life, you start to feel more confident and happier. It is easy to dwell on the aspects of your life that are weighing you down, and that is valid. However, there are also some wonderful aspects about yourself that you could focus on to maximize your true potential. It all starts with loving yourself. The minute you give yourself unconditional love, that is when you will not settle for nothing less than you deserve.

You have been through quite a journey. You have been torn down over and over again and it has taken its toll on you. The toxic person you have been dealing with has ripped you of your identity and autonomy, and you may have neglected your self-worth as a result. You may even find it hard to trust people too. All of your feelings are valid; you have been through so much pain. However, there is still hope for you. Please realize that. All is not lost - now, it is time to turn a new leaf. You are in charge of your life, nobody else. No matter what anyone else says, the remote control is in your hand. Start seeing the things about you that make this world a better place and hone in on them. The world is lucky to have someone as special as you and you should see that for yourself as well. You deserve happiness and love, just like everybody else.

This will not be an easy journey initially, but it will become common practice for you if you are consistent. Even on your hardest days, do not give up. Feel whatever you need to feel, release your emotions. Do not run away from them. That is how you will start to process your wounds and heal. Healing is necessary for you to have a happier life and for that, you need to dig deep and work on yourself from the ground up. Stay informed, enforce your boundaries, practice self-love and grow all the aspects of your life. Focus on YOU. You can do this; you just have to take that brave first step.

Made in the USA
Monee, IL
14 January 2021